D0590820

HOME COURSEBUILDING AND JUMPING

By the same author

THE COURSE BUILDER'S HANDBOOK
(Barrie & Jenkins)

PELHAM HORSEMASTER SERIES

HOME COURSEBUILDING AND JUMPING

Alan Watts

PELHAM BOOKS
LONDON

First published in Great Britain by
Pelham Books Ltd
27 Wrights Lane
London W8 5TZ
1984
Reprinted 1986

British Library Cataloguing in Publication Data

Watts, Alan
   Home coursebuilding and jumping — (Pelham
   horsemaster series)
   1. Show jumping courses — Design and construction
   I. Title
   798.2'5   SF295.5

   ISBN 0 7207 1463 X

Typeset by Cambrian Typesetters, Aldershot
Printed in Great Britain by
Hollen Street Press, Slough
and bound by Hunter & Foulis, Edinburgh.

*To my wife, Joyce, and
my daughter, Christine.*

CONTENTS

FOREWORD
by Lionel Dunning

When I was a kid and had my first pony I used to keep it in the back yard of the butcher's shop that my father owned down in Totton near Southampton. Later we moved and had more land, but even so I had to learn jumping simply by trial and error. Because I have done it all my life I now know by sheer familiarity just what kind of distances I should be setting in combinations etc. for the horses and ponies I am given to ride as I go round talking to people up and down the country.

These things are second nature to me and to people like me who have spent their entire lives around horses and the jumping scene, but not everyone has that kind of experience. They need help with bringing on their young horses and ponies so they can compete on the best possible terms and go on perhaps to Foxhunter and similar classes.

Early training is crucial – it is perhaps the most important thing of all if you want to have a showjumper that will start well and then build up and stay the course. So many people ruin good young stock simply because they get a four-year-old that jumps out of its skin and they jump the poor suffering animal to a point where it starts to refuse . . . and they wonder why. If it weren't so bad for the horse or pony it would serve them right.

One of the very, very important things Alan Watts gets over in his book is that true distances must be graded to the size of your horse or pony and to its stage of training. It is extremely bad to set distances and spreads that are recommended for the most athletic horses and top grade ponies when your own mount is not up to that standard. Once again don't overstretch the animal. If you use the distances given in this book you can develop the horse and not risk later back, and other, troubles.

You mustn't take chances with horses. They are not machines and you must start slowly and develop their muscles gradually. Most great showjumping horses, especially those from German yards, are schooled so that they are fully on the bit before they are ever allowed to compete over fences. There is no substitute for groundwork and I fully endorse what Alan Watts has said on this in his book. The notes on groundwork that Mrs Goldstone has contributed are all sound commonsense and will, if followed, aid you in bringing your young mounts on.

I personally do not like bringing a horse into serious jumping work before it is seven years old, but, of course, that is in the hurly-burly of the big-time, and providing you do not over-face the animals you ride then gymnastic jumping exercises and competitions at the under-four-foot level are well in order.

If you want to have a good and happy horse you will need to have your own little home course and make sure that it is the best you can build. You will also want to alternate your work so the horse does not get bored. I always say to people when I am demonstrating that if a horse refuses a given height or type of obstacle then get off and put the fence down a hole. Don't, whatever you do, go on bashing the poor animal at the same fence at the same height when it obviously is unhappy. Also don't overstretch young horses and ponies over too wide parallels. Again this point is made strongly in this book and is a very good one.

All in all you should be able to build good home courses using the ideas set out by Alan Watts in these pages. I think that the ideas for constructing fences, both coloured and cross-country, are sound and I know that he has actually made these fences because I have seen them and used some of them to build schooling courses when I have been to Colne Valley to run jumping courses.

I started this foreword by recalling my early days with ponies when my friends and I used to hack miles to local shows on the edges of the New Forest. Things were different in the jumping world then. It was much less of a precision game than it is today. That is why I believe that you need the kind of help that Alan Watts is providing in this book. I am glad to be able to say so in this foreword – and I wish you all luck, plus some of the good judgement you should acquire from reading and using *Home Coursebuilding and Jumping.*

Lionel Dunning
October 1983

PREFACE

I have put this book together because I feel there is a need for a more-or-less simple approach to the problems met with by all those who have to build fences and courses at home. By home I mean the field or paddock where you may keep your horse or pony, a site which is often by no means the most ideal for a schooling area. Nevertheless it is all you have and so you use it, but how often do we see the most ghastly conglomerations of old cans, barrels, poles and wings apparently slung together with few of the tenets of good coursebuilding taken into consideration?

I do not blame the messy home coursebuilder — it is hard enough looking after a horse and giving it basic schooling without having to become a coursebuilder as well. Yet just a little extra care could make so much difference, not only to the appearance of the home course, but also to the results when the horse and rider combination goes to local shows.

In this book you will find ideas on how to set out basic exercises and how to work up to bigger things. I have tried to bear in mind the cost of fence material and have assumed that at first you will manage to acquire only a modest quantity of equipment. You will discover, though, that you can accomplish a great deal with a few fences, provided they are properly built and not set up in dangerous ways.

It is very simple to increase your stock of fence-building materials by making certain items yourself and the section on home construction will help in this direction. All the ideas have been tried and been found to work.

I am certain that if you learn some of the art of coursebuilding at home you will be far more able to see the problems that professional coursebuilders will set you when you go away from home. However, it is a fact of life that horse people do not care much for numbers. Calculations are something for the classroom, not for the stables. Therefore, because good course-building is a question of distances and heights and getting the combination and related distances 'true', I have striven to relieve the reader of any drudgery in that direction.

I have calculated for ponies and horses the true distances that should be set in combinations and you will find that when the fences get large, and the horses likewise, then my figures tend to become those recom-mended by the British Show Jumping Association. However, as novice animals will not be jumping great heights, nor will they have the build of the big show-jumpers, they will need shorter true distances. The tables allow for these factors.

Wherever the word 'horse' appears you may have to read 'horse or pony'. To have constantly written 'horse or pony' would have become tedious, and I think un-necessary.

I have written this book in Imperial units of feet and inches for two reasons. The first is that most people who will use it will naturally think in feet and inches. Secondly most showjumping material bought from saddlery companies will be made to Imperial standards and not to metric ones. Conversions into metric are given at the end of the book.

Because this book is more concerned with the techni-calities of building fences there is not a vast amount of advice on how to jump the fences, but I have been lucky enough to have the help and assistance of an inspired teacher of riding, Mrs Diana Goldstone. Where there are notes on schooling the rider and the horse over fences then, to a large degree, these are based on her writing and advice.

Some of the ideas set out in the book first saw print in the magazines *Horse and Rider* and *Pony*, and I would like to thank their respective editors Julia Goodwin and Nancy Roberts for allowing me to first air my material in their pages.

I want to also thank Mike Roberts, owner of the Colne Valley Riding Stables, who has given me free rein to develop outdoor and indoor jumping courses, and who has provided the financial wherewithal to do it. When you have to build up from literally nothing then you learn a great deal and the experience gained has helped fill these pages.

Finally I must thank Lionel Dunning for generously agreeing to write a foreword. His methods with his big showjumpers are often applicable to lesser horses and so things I have learned from him are also incorporated.

All in all I hope this book will open a few doors to better coursebuilding and jumping at home.

July 1983

PREFACE TO THE SECOND IMPRINT

Because of its very basic nature there is nothing that I feel needs changing in the text. However there has been a welcome move on the part of the British Show Jumping Association to bring their officially recommended distances to be set in combinations down by a substantial margin. Thus they conform much more closely to the distances that I calculated using ideas set out in Appendix 2 and which allowed for horse size, fence size and speed of approach. I have found with further experience no real need to alter the distances given in the tables herein. They may differ somewhat from the BSJA recommended distances, but they are after all for novice horses. In training your horse to enter BSJA competitions note must be taken of the distances given in Appendix 1 as these are the ones they will meet.

Alan Watts
November 1986

INTRODUCTION
Preparing for Jumping

If you are one of the majority you will start your jumping career by going to local shows and gymkhanas. Many of these are well run and have properly constructed courses, but there are some where the most elementary of course-building rules fly out of the window. In any case even at some high-class shows the clear-round course is often quite awful because the person running it has had to make do with material left over from the main rings.

Over these unfortunate fences even more unfortunate horses and ponies are made to jump. Nothing is going to change this situation and therefore, you may say, if you are expected to jump a badly constructed course away from home then you can get by with the same thing when you *are* at home. This would be a valid point if you did not wish to progress, but hopefully this is not the case.

After competing at the local shows you will want to try your hand at bigger unaffiliated events elsewhere and eventually the affiliated circuits. Then things become quite different. If your horse has not been properly schooled on the flat so that he is supple and balanced on both reins and can strike off on the correct leg, nor carefully encouraged to jump uprights, spreads, walls and planks and enjoy the experience, he is going to start refusing and running out when the heights reach 3ft 6ins and above. Within reason a horse with an average amount of muscle can take 3ft 6ins in his stride, but add 6 inches or more and immediately the showjumpers become separated from the 'also-rans'.

Early training is perhaps the most important thing in a happy horse's life. If he is brought on with care and consideration and not over-faced by the rider (who cannot wait to get into the show ring) he can go on developing towards higher things as his physique and experience grow. Experience on the part of the rider, or the riding instructor, can sometimes retrieve the form of a horse that has been hopelessly spoiled in its early training, but it is so much better that progress should be steady and gradual rather than a tidal regime of apparently flooding successes followed by ebbing fortunes as horse and rider find they have been insufficiently prepared to meet their match when the fences get big.

Nothing is going to make up for the careful coaching by an experienced instructor both on the flat and over the jumps, but many people cannot find the means to take their horses to a good teacher and therefore they have to do most of the work themselves. However, if you want to jump consistent clear rounds there is no short cut — even a top showjumper may not click with a horse until he or she has spent a long and heart-breaking time reaching a level of understanding, and why should you be any different?

The first basic preparation for going to shows is groundwork, the long arduous hours of preliminary dressage which so often prove to you that you cannot ride. You cannot really do this adequately on your own despite some of the good books there are to help you. You need the tutelage of a first-rate instructor, someone you trust and admire for his or her abilities and flair for extracting better and better performances out of you and your horse.

An hour's lesson a week will not be enough. You will have to go home or to your livery stable and work on what you have been taught. But unless you discipline yourself to do this the early success you think you have found, when your horse, with natural ability, jumps clear rounds over 3ft fences, is going to disappear when the fences get considerably higher.

The instruction you receive may include elementary jumping and that is good because groundwork and jumping go hand in hand, but, dare I say it, if you cannot afford both flatwork and jumping lessons then opt for flatwork as successful jumping is far more likely to be accomplished on your own.

So you must set up at home the best courses you can consistent with what you have available and you should aim to build your home courses with the same attention to detail as good professional coursebuilders bring to their art. Help in doing this is to be found in the following pages.

Along with your flatwork you need to start the novice horse over trotting poles and cavalletti to enable him to find his feet and yourself to maintain a consistent balance. You can then progress to low jumps and to certain gymnastic exercises to improve the combined coordination of horse and rider.

Horses will more readily jump fences that are well-constructed than they will ghastly erections of wood and tin cans which so often seem to serve for home schooling. Fences should look solid so that the horse will respect them. An experienced horse will jump single poles suspended over nothing, but for more novice horses and for larger fences such a construction is quite unsuitable.

During a lecture a top coursebuilder recently described himself, I hope in jest, as 'the laziest coursebuilder in the world'. Now this may be true because he has considerable resources of men and material behind him, but such a situation will not apply to you, and you will not do yourself or your horse justice if you are also numbered amongst the laziest of home coursebuilders.

It may seem a chore having to think out and construct a course appropriate for your stage of training but it is as essential as cleaning your tack or riding 20-metre circles.

You will not use or need all the ideas in this book, but they will aid you in efficiently preparing your horse for the local shows and stand you in good stead for when you start in the big-time.

PART ONE

BASIC FENCE-BUILDING
AND JUMPING

1 MAKING A START

Straw Bales

Straw-bale fences can look awful, but with a little trouble they can provide extra fences in a sparsely equipped jumping paddock.

It is of course possible to make a simple fence by laying a pole across a couple of bales arranged as wings, but unless you have another pole that is shorter, you cannot lay one vertically below it for a groundline. Further, you cannot alter the height. One bale is often too low while two, stacked on top of one another, are too high.

The only way you can obtain a groundline is to place a pole in front of the bales as shown in Fig. 1 (a) and (b). If you do this you run the risk of the horse hitting the pole, rolling it and landing astride it. It is not at all a good way of doing things.

If you intend to set up some bales for a cheap and convenient jump then the pole has to be laid on the end of the bales as shown in Fig. 1 (c). If you want a parallel it is tempting to lay two poles on bales as in Fig. 1 (d), but a hard rap on the first one can roll it into the second one, which again can be dangerous.

You can set up some really good fences with bales if you use bale cups. These are easy to make and enable you to construct safe, simple fences with plenty of variations in shape and height.

The method of making the cups is covered in the building section at the back of the book (see page 155) Photo 1 gives a close-up of how they should be used.

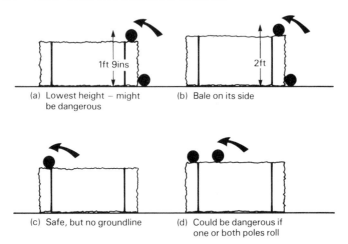

(a) Lowest height – might be dangerous

1ft 9ins

(b) Bale on its side

2ft

(c) Safe, but no groundline

(d) Could be dangerous if one or both poles roll

Fig.1 *Using bales on their own is very restricting and can be dangerous when poles are rolled but cannot fall. One bale height may be too low and two too high.*

You can see two kinds here. At the back is a simple cup which can be sandwiched between bales giving only the height of a bale. However, rather than having the pole laid on the edge of the bales, the pole is in a real cup out of which it can be knocked, and a pole of the same length can be laid below it as a groundline.

To achieve variation in height build cups similar to the one just described but nail a notched block of wood securely to them as shown in the foreground of Photo 1 and described on page 156. You can then place poles at intermediate heights that would never have been possible using bales alone. With bale cups of the design above you can set up the following heights using standard bales:

Set in a stack of:

2 bales	a simple cup	gives about	1ft 9 ins or 2ft 0ins
2 bales	a blocked cup	gives about	2ft 3ins or 2ft 6ins
3 bales	a simple cup	gives about	3ft 3ins or 3ft 6ins
3 bales	a blocked cup	gives about	3ft 9ins or 4ft 0ins

With the groundline pole set in front of the leading element of an ascending parallel you have the first approach to a triple bar, and if you set your groundline in hollow blocks as described on page 35, or on something else that is not too far off the ground, you have a more classic triple bar.

Opposite: Photo 1 *Bale cups in use making an ascending parallel. Bright attractive fillers can be formed from plastic containers as shown here.*

Here is what is required to build different fences:

Number of bales	Number of poles	Simple cups	Blocked cups	Shape of Fence	Height
4	2	2	0	Upright	1ft 9 ins
6	3	4	0	Upright	3ft 3ins
4	2	0	2	Upright	2ft 3ins
4	3	2	2(upper)	Ascending //	2ft 3ins
6	3	2	2(lower)	Ascending //	3ft 3ins
4	3	4	0	True //	2ft 0ins
4	3	0	4	True //	2ft 6 ins (2ft spread)
6	3	4	0	True //	3ft 6ins

(// means parallel)

Poles

Whatever you use for the wings in your embryonic jump-ing course you must have poles. Poles sold by saddlery companies are either plain wood with the bark taken off, or painted. The latter cost quite a bit more and so you may wish to paint the poles yourself. Ready-painted poles often have a few wide strips of colour rather than the more useful pattern of evenly spaced bands of about a foot wide. Thus painting your own can be advantageous.

Poles bought from tack-shops etc. are usually either 12ft or 10ft long to accord with the requirements of full-sized courses, but you do not need them that long. A very good length is 9ft, for several reasons. They are easier to handle; and because most rough poles taper, the shorter length means that the difference between the thickness of the two ends is smaller and they will therefore look much better. Another advantage of the odd-number length is that if you paint nine 1ft wide stripes on them you have colour at both ends. With 10ft or 12ft poles painted with 1ft bands you end up with a coloured band at one end and a white one at the other. So in order to get a coloured band at both ends, you have to make your bands just over 13ins wide.

With 9ft poles you can build fences in smaller spaces than you can with the longer lengths, and the poles are correspondingly cheaper. However, the idea of 9ft poles may not have filtered through to your supplier, but if you have an outpost of the Forestry Commission nearby you may be able to buy poles straight from the forest and do the whole thing yourself. In this case you could probably buy poles that are 18ft or more long and cut them in two with little wastage.

If you decide to make your own poles from newly-felled wood you must expect to put in some hard work. The poles need to be bought in the autumn and allowed to dry out under cover through the winter. Then they have to be stripped of their bark and the knots planed or sawn off before the poles are cut to length and given a priming coat of paint. If you cannot afford wood primer then a white emulsion paint provides a serviceable undercoat. Some lengths can be left as rustic poles, which cuts down the work, but the majority need to be painted so that, as they say in the advertisements, your mount 'has seen coloured poles'.

When the emulsion is fully dry, mark out the width of the bands. Make them a foot wide so that you can use the poles as measures in your schooling, as described later. On a 9ft pole you obviously will mark out nine 1ft widths; on a 10ft pole you will either mark out nine bands of $13\frac{1}{3}$ ins if you want colour both ends, or ten bands of 12ins if you are not worried that the end band is a colour at one end and white at the other. The same goes for a 12ft pole: eleven bands that are 13.1ins wide will give colour both ends, and twelve bands of a foot will give colour and white.

If you want the edges of the coloured stripes to look sharp then bind masking tape where the colour needs to end, having previously roughly painted the white bands with gloss paint and allowed it to dry. Note that masking tape is always put on within the white bands.

If you want your course to look good as well as serviceable do not paint rainbow hues on your poles. Several colours on a pole look cheap and nasty — more fitting to a fairground than to a jumping ring. Choose a bright colour you like and make sure that at least four of your poles will be the same colour. Then when you add to your stock of poles, buy or paint several poles of another, contrasting, colour. Pillar-box or signal red is a colour with which you cannot go wrong, and a holly or Buckingham green is also good. Blues should be bright but at the same time muted; royal blue is not good as it is very vivid and navy blue is too dark. There are many deep blues on the market that are excellent for painted poles. You can have a set of four rustic poles as well as a set of coloured poles when you are first building up, but a whole course of rustic poles is a very drab affair altogether.

An easy addition to your stock of poles is afforded by making a stile as outlined in the construction section on page 157. Here you have only to buy three or four 9ft lengths of 3ins x 3ins planed timber and take off the sharp edges with a plane or a Surform. The rails can then be painted with white undercoat plus a gloss coat.

You will need to put the rails in stile cups (as shown on page 157) because they cannot be placed in standard round cups. However, you could, if necessary, lay the rails on standard flat cups. As cups will be at a premium on most home courses and stile cups are very easy to make, you can save money on cups by including a stile in your home training courses.

Cups

Standard cups come in two kinds — round and flat. Most people acquire the round ones in the preliminary stages of buying their home jumping equipment. Cups come with pins made of $^3/_8$ in. diameter metal, and as a cup without a pin is useless, it is essential at the outset to tie the pins securely to the holes provided in the cups with a short length of thick string.

It is fairly unlikely that you will try to make your own standard cups, but, if you should, Fig. 2 shows how they are constructed. The centres of holes drilled in uprights to take standard cups must be $1^5/_8$ ins from the face of the upright. Page 167 expalins how you can drill these yourself.

If you intend to use planks on your home course — and you certainly should — you will need flat cups to

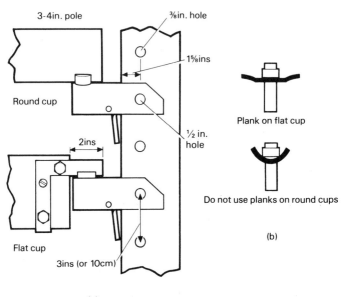

Fig. 2(a) *The critical dimensions of round and flat cups to fit standard uprights.*
(b) *Resting planks on round cups is a lazy and dangerous practice.*

rest them on. There may be a temptation to make do with the round ones you already have — and does it matter anyway?

Well, you can rest planks in round cups if you like, but if you do they will not come off if knocked. Some will say that is a good thing for it will teach the horse to pick his feet up the next time. That may be so, but the horse that raps a plank set in round cups may hit it so hard that he:

(i) damages himself;

(ii) breaks a plank — unless they are very stout;

(iii) knocks over one or both of the wings.

In any case the practice is bad. Your horse will be under

the impression that he can rap planks and they will stay put and when he gets to a show where the course is built properly the first thing he will do is knock the planks down.

If you want a plank fence without the expense of several pairs of flat cups, you could use just one plank as the top element of the fence with poles or possibly hurdles underneath. That way you would need just one pair of flat cups. The splendid all-plank uprights seen at better shows are built that way for aesthetic reasons — as far as the horse is concerned the top plank is the only one that counts.

You will need more than one set of flat cups for any gates you wish to include in your course and the remarks about not using round cups apply even more to a heavy gate than they do to a light plank.

Having mentioned gates this is a good point to warn against leaning gates at an angle to the ground when you want a lower height than the gate will allow. This is acceptable if you lay the gate against the direction of jumping and not with it (Fig. 62 shows why).

Simple Fillers

For even the most basic of home courses you will need fillers. In Photo 2 versatile fillers are afforded by cans that have been painted and carefully vetted to ensure that they do not exude dangerous chemicals. With its three-tier wings the ascending parallel shown makes a good, solid-looking fence.

If you want to use bales as fillers then of course they can be used plain, but by painting shapes on lengths of wallpaper and wrapping these round the bales (Photo 3) horses can be introduced to some of the strange patterns that are to be found on jump fillers at shows. It is amazing how just a little effort transforms an untidy heap of straw into a useful fence. If you want to leave

Photo 2 *While four bales will suffice for the wings, six will give a more solid appearance. A set of cans, laid as shown, make an acceptable filler, but they should be restrained from rolling if hit by having a pole laid close to them on the ground on this side.*

these fillers out in the wet then painting the shapes onto plastic bags is a good idea.

Finding items to fill homemade fences is always a problem. You could consider stuffing old plastic sacks with old hay or fodder that cannot be used and laying the bags in the bottom of the fence as shown in Photo 4. If all you can find are paper sacks they you will have to bring them in after use in case of rain.

Photo 3 *A more formidable fence — a true parallel filled with straw bales and unfamiliar shapes painted on wallpaper and slid under the bale twine.*

Photo 4 *Sacks stuffed with straw or old fodder make good fillers and save on poles and cups.*

2 USING TROTTING POLES AND CAVALLETTI

The strides of ponies and horses are very different and it is essential to start novice animals over trotting poles set at distances that they can easily negotiate. 'Baby' horses have great difficulty in coming to grips with where their feet are when they are asked to trot down a line of poles and it takes a good deal of practice before they can do it efficiently.

Here is a table of true distances at which to set the trotting poles depending on the size of pony/horse:

	12.2 hh	13.2 hh	14.2 hh	15.2 hh	16.2 hh
Trotting	3 ft	3ft 3ins	3ft 6ins	4ft	4ft 6ins
Cantering	4ft 3ins	4ft 6ins	4ft 9ins	5ft 6ins	6ft 3ins

As its training proceeds you want your horse to be able to shorten and lengthen its stride and so these distances can be varied up and down by about 6ins.

A normal stride for an average person is nothing like 3ft. It is, for example, 2ft 6ins in my own case and I am 5ft 8ins tall. It takes me quite a giant stride to cover 3ft. Thus simple paces will not give the above distances very easily and all you can do is use one or two of your own paces as a guide and adjust the trotting poles accordingly. You can mark the basic distances on your true distance scale as described on page 67.

One of the biggest practical problems with home schooling is that usually there is no one to help you replace any jumps or trotting poles which may have been knocked down or stumbled over. In this book you will find several suggestions towards helping with these problems and so minimise the number of times you have to dismount in a schooling session. The first of these ideas involves:

Concrete Cavalletti

These are effective, inexpensive schooling aids which utilise the square, hollow building blocks that can be bought from builders' merchants. These blocks might have been designed to take normal-thickness poles, and although they may be rather heavy to move therein lies their effectiveness. While a really hard rap from a horse's hoof will move them, under most circumstances they will stay put. This eliminates having to dismount several times during a session and it also means that you can arrange the distances accurately at the start and expect them to remain the same.

The distances between poles are laid out using the same set of measuring poles as used to create the true distance scale, page 67. Choose as flat a piece of ground as you can and set out the blocks along the scale. It is not important how wide the lane is and poles considerably shorter than those used for fences can be utilised. You can use old coloured poles that are past their best, or even broken poles. Whatever poles you use they should be coloured so that the horse can see them properly and have less chance of hitting them.

Building blocks are sold either as singles or doubles. While the double ones shown in Fig. 3 (a) would seem useful for obtaining more height when required, they are too heavy to lift easily and tend to topple if not supported either side. It is best to buy a dozen or so

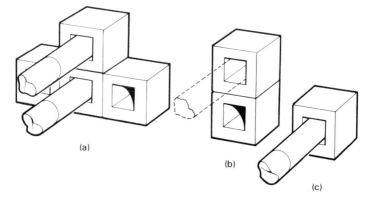

Fig. 3 *Using building block cavalletti.* (a) *If double blocks are used they need supporting and are also very heavy.* (b) *Two single blocks placed on top of one another are often better.* (c) *This height is useful for trotting poles.*

single blocks and they can then be stacked as in Fig. 3 (b) or used singly as in Fig. 3 (c). If you paint them white they look smart and can double as dressage-arena markers. You can set them out as shown on page 45.

A dozen blocks – eight with the appropriate letters on, plus four for marking the corners – make a stable and permanent dressage arena which can, when you have ridden a groove in the turf, be easily moved. Obviously if you want to leave your dressage arena semi-permanently in place you cannot use the same blocks for cavalletti. If schooling for flatwork and jumping are to go on together you will need up to twenty-four blocks. However, these blocks are so versatile they will not prove a bad investment and their cost is small compared, say, to buying ready-made cavalletti or dressage markers.

Wooden Cavalletti

For cheapness, versatility and effect the concrete cavalletti described above offer an effective answer to the problem of schooling over small obstacles. However, you may wish to have the traditional form of wooden cavalletti and so dimensions etc. are given here.

There are two forms of bar that can be used: 7—8ft lengths of either rustic poles (Fig. 4 (a)) or 3ins x 3ins planed wooden bars (Fig. 4 (b)).

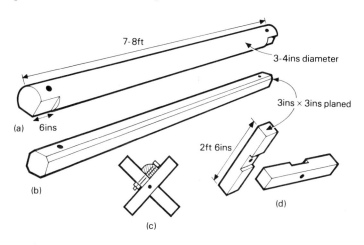

Fig. 4 *Dimensions and construction details for wooden cavalletti.*

In the case of rustic poles, cut flats on either end as shown, and, when you have made the cross-arms out of two 2ft 6in. lengths of 3ins x 3ins timber and bolted them together with 5in. bolts, bolt the pole through one cross-arm as shown in Fig. 4 (c). Cavalletti have to withstand a great deal of punishment and so must be rigidly constructed. This is why it is essential to slot the two arms into one another as shown in Fig. 4 (d). Failing that, you can overcome this carpentry job by using a good glue (see page 151) between the two arms when you bolt them up.

If you want to use a 3ins x 3ins planed wooden bar as shown in Fig. 4 (b) then you must take the trouble to chamfer off the sharp edges or the horse could cut himself. Once again bolt the bar to the cross-arms making sure to obtain a neat fit to maintain strength. You will need 6in. bolts for this job. If you are using glue, also glue the edges of the bar to the appropriate bits of the cross-arms which will all add to the strength.

A single cavalletto is not much use by itself so while you are making one you should make three, or two at the very least. They pay for their construction by being one more aid to building obstacles around a small home jumping course.

Exercises

Negotiating trotting poles laid on the ground or fixed in building blocks, as described on page 36, is a good exercise for any horse or pony whatever its stage of training. For the young horse trotting pole exercises are an essential pre-requisite to training in jumping. It is very important that the horse can trot through a set of, say, five poles laid out at the correct distances, in a smooth and balanced manner. Many quite experienced horses find difficulty in negotiating the poles without hitting them and this indicates that they are not sufficiently aware of the position of their feet. Lack of coordination and balance on the part of the rider contribute significantly to this problem.

To make a basic trotting lane you will need five poles plus ten blocks, or five cavalletti, plus measuring poles. For a simple straight lane the layout is simply an extension of that shown in Photo 5. By using measuring poles it is easy to set the poles at the correct distance for the size of horse/pony. If the distances are not quite exact it does not matter — it makes a useful problem for the horse. However, there should not be too much

Photo 5 *Using concrete cavalletti. Note the measuring poles down the side to facilitate laying out the distances. The final cavalletto is set in a double block, but experience has shown that this is easily knocked over and needs support as in Fig. 3.*

variation between one distance and the next. If you intend to shorten or lengthen the distances they should *all* be shortened or lengthened as this helps build rhythm into the exercise. If you have enough poles leave the measuring ones where they are for quick, easy readjustment of the distances.

Basic distances are given at the start of this section, but with experience the distances can be shortened by, say, 3 inches. Once the horse negotiates the poles calmly and rhythmically then the last cavalletto can be

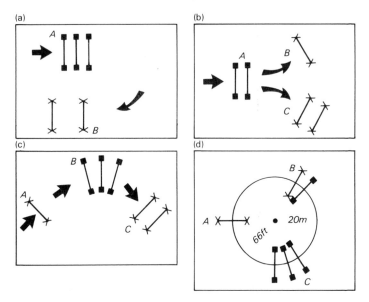

Fig. 5 *Suggestions for various exercises. (See text for details.)*

replaced by a low fence. However, before attempting this, try some of the cavalletti exercises outlined in Fig. 5:

Fig. 5 (a) *A* is a set of trotting poles followed by a turn. Later establish canter on the turn and ride over two cavalletti (*B*) set at cantering distance. Do this on both reins.

Fig. 5 (b) is an exercise in controlled riding into jumps. *A* will regulate the horse's pace before the turn into a single cavalletto (*B*) or a small spread (*C*) of two cavalletti.

Fig. 5 (c) is a more difficult exercise to be undertaken at trot. The 'fan' of trotting poles (set with their centres at trotting distances) should be ridden both where they are wider and where they are narrower. This is followed by a pair of cavalletti whose height can be varied with experience.

Fig. 5 (d) is a 'continuous' exercise on a 20-metre (66ft) circle. As shown the exercise should be ridden *A—C—B* as *B* makes a low ascending parallel. Reverse the groundline pole of *B* on the other rein.

You can vary the above exercises as you wish, providing you keep an eye on the distances between the elements.

Schooling Hints

Ridden exercises, whether on the flat or involving poles and obstacles, should follow a progressive plan. This will help you detect faults in yourself and your horse, and you can correct them before they escalate and become permanent problems. Whatever standard you and your horse are working at there are many exercises involving series of poles, cavalletti and small obstacles which will benefit you both. This athletic work will:

(1) give the young horse confidence by teaching him to adjust and match his balance to his length of stride;

(2) keep the jumping horse or pony alert and athletic;

(3) prevent dressage or show animals becoming 'stodgy' and mechanical;

(4) help develop suppleness and a feeling of being 'with' the horse. This is particularly useful for the novice rider where the continuity of a series of poles and/or obstacles will sharpen reactions and coordination of the aids.

Your ability to remain in balance with, and ride your horse positively, yet calmly, forward is crucial. Make sure you ride in a jumping position with stirrups shortened to close your knee snugly into the knee-roll of the saddle. To ensure you remain with your horse bend forward from the hip (not from the waist or you will lose your balance) so that you absorb the movement of the horse. Keep your back flat and try to retain a steady

Photo 6 *Using cavalletti on the turn. This is a good exercise because it automatically makes the pony shorten or lengthen his stride depending on whether he is ridden nearer or further from the centre of the poles. The 'poles' shown here are in fact stile rails, i.e. 9ft lengths of 3in. x 3in. planed wood.*

'elastic' contact with the horse's mouth.

Before you begin any gymnastic exercises, have your horse working as well as possible on the flat. Ride turns, circles, changes of direction and transitions from one pace to another.

As you approach the poles make sure the horse is straight and working energetically. When passing over the poles do not pull back on the reins or drop the contact but allow the horse to stretch his neck if he wishes. Keep your legs on his sides but do not actually push him on unless he loses impetus. The horse must learn for himself how to negotiate the obstacles in front of him. Ride over the poles in both directions and off both reins. Increase the number of poles and vary the distances with care.

If at any point during the exercises your horse becomes over-excited, worried or nappy and you are unsure why, consider the following suggestions:

(1) You may have asked too much of him all at once. Maybe the horse is unfit and feels tired.

(2) Check your saddle and bridle. Is your bit too strong? Is the martingale or noseband too tight? Does the saddle or girth cause pressure or pinch? All these will upset the horse.

(3) Does the horse respond willingly to your leg aids or does he hang back unless you use your legs hard? If he does not listen to your leg aids, support them with a few taps of a schooling whip used close to and simultaneously with a lighter leg aid than you usually use. Once you have corrected the horse do not go back to using strong leg aids or you will not have improved him. Make sure you use the lower leg in an inward and forward manner, not back and up raising the heel.

Look at your rein contact. Do you have a direct line to your horse's mouth or do the reins have a loose-tight, loose-tight action? Are your hands too close together or is one or both of your wrists not rounded enough? The above faults will make the horse feel as if he cannot move freely forward. He will feel restricted through his shoulders and no amount of pushing with your legs will help him.

3 SETTING OUT AND USING A SCHOOLING AREA

While this is a book about jumping at home it is most important to do a correct proportion of work on the flat and therefore hints on setting out a small schooling arena and suggestions on what to work on are offered here. It is fully accepted that good consistent jumping follows from obedience training on the flat and so jumping and flatwork have to go hand-in-hand with an emphasis on the latter.

A small dressage arena is two 20-metre (66ft) squares put together (Fig. 6). The diagonal markers are 6 metres (19½ft) in from the corners, but it is not absolutely necessary to set a perfectly exact size when schooling. Set out your arena with normal paces using the table below.

Personal stride	132ft	d	66ft
1ft 9ins	75	84	38
2ft	66	74	33
2ft 3ins	59	66	29
2ft 6ins	53	59	26
2ft 9ins	48	54	24
3ft	44	49	22

Site the arena on as level a piece of ground as possible and clear up any small holes and stones etc. You can mark out the area with eight of the hollow building blocks mentioned earlier. Paint the letters A, K, E, H,

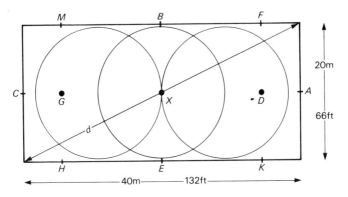

Fig. 6 *The basic dressage arena.*

C, M, B, F on these in black, having first painted the blocks white. Alternatively, plastic containers or cans filled with water or sand could be utilised. Whatever you use must stay put, regardless of the weather. The letters follow the mnemonic

A Keen Efficient Horse Can Make Beautiful Form

clockwise round the arena, from the entrance at A.

It is customary to make white wooden corner markers, but they are not essential as the white blocks, or other markers, will delineate the shape quite adequately.

For practical reasons the positions G, X and D cannot be marked and must be located relative to the side markers.

Riding a horse properly is a great art and while books help they cannot make up for the attentions of a trusted teacher. This book does not even pretend to teach all you should know about schooling your horse on the flat or over fences, but it provides ideas on what should be aimed at with hints on how to correct the most common faults. Experience shows that very often you cannot correct single-handedly a fault that has developed and you will have to seek professional advice.

Here are a few of the more common problems you may encounter and with which you will usually need help:

(1) Wrong leg position, which will prevent you making a consistent contact with the horse's sides and at the same time develop the wrong riding muscles. Included here are legs too far forward and toes too turned out. Equally bad is legs too far back, so pushing backwards and upwards rather than forwards and upwards. This tends to confuse the horse.

(2) Leaning too far forward or backward thus not being in balance with the horse. You may have great problems with this unless you have someone knowledgeable on the ground correcting your position. The forward seat is adopted for jumping, but in basic schooling on the flat you should feel that the whole weight of the body is going vertically down the spine into the seat.

(3) Leaning to one side or the other, and particularly to the inside of a turn or circle, causes the horse to lose balance. Riding a horse round a bend is not like riding a bike. You should not lean in but sit upright as normal. The horse can then independently lean in the amount he knows is correct for negotiating the degree of bend (which he has learned during periods of freedom). Thus he maintains balance and rhythm without interference from his rider.

(4) Failure to follow the movements of the horse's head and neck through having the arms and wrists too rigid. The horse's head acts as a heavy balance weight and he must be able to use it as such especially when jumping or performing gymnastic exercises. Having rounded wrists aids this sympathetic following of the horse's head motion when on the flat. Giving a more-or-less free rein (without actually dropping the contact) during the last non-jumping and take-off strides when jumping,

helps to achieve that primary aim of all advanced riding — to give the horse the feeling that while you have control he can still perform all those beautiful, natural movements of which he is capable when free in the paddock. (5) Under the above head comes bad rein contact, including reins that are of unequal length leading to uneven pressure on parts of the mouth. When a horse carries his head at an angle to the vertical, especially when riding through corners, correction can often be achieved by raising the rein opposite to the direction of the head. However, this is only an aid directed towards building up the muscles that will produce a correct head carriage and the eventual aim is to ride calmly with the reins at an equal height and with a straight line from elbow to bit.

Having looked at some of the more common problems/faults, here are some useful exercises to try:

(1) Ride through the corners on both reins working towards achieving a symmetrical bend in the horse's head and neck. The horse cannot bend throughout its length as there is very little, if any, lateral flexibility in the spine. Thus when an advanced horse appears to bend throughout its length this is an illusion produced with the help of considerable impulsion of the inside hind leg and flexion of the neck. The hind legs must follow exactly in the track of the forelegs round the curve and the animal's quarters must not be allowed to drift outward, a common fault in many horses. Restraining pressure must be applied by using your outside leg placed a little further back than the inside one. ('Outside' and 'inside' refer to the outside and inside of the curve you are riding.)

You must not expect too much of a horse at first. The period of schooling that most people, who cannot ride full-time, require to produce a reasonable degree of suppleness must be measured in years and not in months. Devices which attempt to produce quick results with a horse's head carriage must be used only as temporary aids and abandoned as soon as some improvement is shown. Over a period of time these contrivances force the horse to use and develop muscles which he would not naturally develop. Having been produced, the muscles may never quite return to that state of development which would have been achieved following a long period of more acceptable natural schooling. There are very few short-cuts to more advanced riding — only more knowledge and more self-discipline.

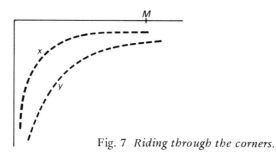

Fig. 7 *Riding through the corners.*

Referring to Fig. 7, a young horse can be expected to walk through a bend such as (y) with something approaching the right degree of flexion. At trot he will almost certainly throw his head out to the side in an attempt to maintain his balance. With time the horse can be trotted round (y) and eventually cantered through this curve. It will take an advanced horse to negotiate the curve (x) at trot with a correct bend and in balance. Cantering bends such as (x) is an exercise for top dressage horses.

(2) Ride straight lines both along the long and short sides and, importantly, up and down the centre line. Concentrate on absolute straightness. For example at A line up a marker behind C and concentrate on keeping

the two in line. You should be able to correct slight deviations from the straight line that occur by putting more weight in the opposite seat-bone.

Common faults include riding with the quarters 'in' or 'out', i.e. to left or right when on the left rein and vice versa when on the opposite rein. You must aim to create power in the hindquarters and allow this power to flow through into a restraining contact. Thus starts the journey towards collection by inducing the horse to bring his hind legs more under his body thus transferring some of his weight off his forehand. The forehand can only be 'lightened' when some degree of collection (i.e. engagement of the hindquarters) has been achieved. When the horse is supple on both reins and has progressed to a degree of collection the problems of quarters 'in' or 'out' will disappear. As a variation ride straight lines off the sides, i.e. *K* to *M* etc. and also from *A* to *E* and *A* to *B* etc.

(3) Ride 20-metre circles which occupy the full width of the arena as shown in Fig. 6. It is best to learn to walk a true circle at first as it is quite difficult to maintain a constant radius of curve without falling in towards the centre or otherwise falling out. Aim to achieve the correct bend in the horse and when you have gained some success at the walk move up to trot and eventually to canter.

(4) Ride linked 10-metre semi-circles (Fig. 8). These are ridden at walk in preliminary dressage, but later at trot. Start the semi-circle from *B* or *E* a few paces further on than the marker so that you can ride a few straight steps through *X* before commencing the circle on the opposite rein.

(5) Ride changes of direction which can include:

   (a) diagonal changes from quarter marker to quarter marker;
   (b) riding out of a 20-metre circle;

(c) changing direction within the circle;

(d) performing some demi-volte changes of rein — for example ride from *H* to *E*, and at *E* ride two thirds of a 10-metre circle on the left rein then bring the horse back onto the track near to *H*;

(e) changing the rein by half-school turns across the arena from *E* to *B* or *B* to *E*. The inside leg must be very active here in order to prevent the horse's quarters falling in.

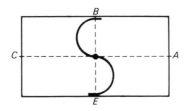

Fig. 8 *Linked 10-metre semi-circles.*

4 PRELIMINARY JUMPING EXERCISES

Once you and your horse have mastered the trotting poles, you can then move on to work with a grid of cavalletti or low jumps of about 9 inches high. If using concrete blocks you will need two stacked on top of one another to get the extra height and there may be problems with the unevenness of the ground. Fig. 9 shows a grid of five elements but it is not necessary to have so many. It is a good idea to start with two or three and add more, one at a time.

Fig. 9 *Setting out trotting poles or a low grid.*

With experience change the distance x between the elements from those given on page 34 as follows:

	13.2 hh	14.2 hh	15.2 hh	16.2 hh
At trot	3ft	3ft 3ins	3ft 9ins	4ft 3ins
At canter	4ft 6ins	4ft 9ins	5ft 6ins	6ft 3ins

Aim to trot and canter these grids in a controlled but active manner and expect the horse to use himself. So long as it is not overdone, a sharp tap with the whip can be employed if the horse is lazy. However, if you cannot maintain your own balance do not expect the horse to do likewise. This is an exercise in coordination for both rider and horse.

Exercise 1 You are now in a position to add a low jump at the end of the grid. To begin with you may find that four cavalletti before the fence (set at about 1ft 6ins high) are too many. Adjust the distance *y* in front of the fence to conform to your horse's height as follows:

Cantering	13.2 hh	14.2 hh	15.2 hh	16.2 hh
Distance *y*	6ft	6ft 6ins	7ft 3ins	8ft 3ins

The grid will look like this:

Fig. 10 *Exercise 1 — three cavalletti and a low jump.*

This exercise is a simple extension of the grid of trotting poles already outlined and, at first, with a young horse, just one distance *x* and then a small jump will be hard enough. The horse will have to think where his feet are and the rider will have to keep the forward impulsion through the grid even though the 'young' horse may stumble.

Exercise 2 The degree of difficulty can now be increased by using two small jumps but retaining the regulating cavalletti. The distance *z* between the jumps should be as follows:

Cantering	13.2 hh	14.2 hh	15.2 hh	16.2 hh
Distance z	7ft 6ins	8ft	8ft 9ins	10ft

The exercise is not concerned with jumping height, but is to teach the horse and rider to approach the fences in a calm manner. This way the young horse learns where its feet are, but equally the rider must concentrate on thinking where the horse's feet are.

Fig. 11 *Exercise 2 — two cavalletti and two low jumps.*

Exercise 3 When such exercises as these can be tackled with some fluency you are in a position to go for more height. In this case 'height' means about 2ft or 2ft 3ins — a level you know you can do with ease.

Set out the exercise with y and z as above and add a higher fence at the distance a as follows:

Cantering	13.2 hh	14.2 hh	15.2 hh	16.2 hh
Distance a	8ft 6ins	9ft	10ft	11ft 6ins

Fig. 12 *Exercise 3 — cavalletto followed by two low jumps and a larger fence.*

Preparatory Canter Work

Once you start actually jumping fences from a canter any problems you may have had on the flat or in the early pole-work are likely to put in an appearance again.

The canter should be active and forward going. To assess and improve on the canter, make alterations within the pace as follows: try to obtain three or four different speeds, then improve the quality of each by asking the horse to step his hindlegs further under his body without increasing his speed.

Work at each canter speed over grids of poles and cavalletti and alter the distances between the poles to suit the strides. Canter on straight lines, turns and circles.

The purpose of canter work over series of poles and small obstacles is:

(1) to teach the horse to take each obstacle in his stride;
(2) to establish his canter more positively and improve upon his physical and mental capabilities;
(3) to build up the horse and rider partnership.

If your horse has difficulty maintaining the canter, particularly throughout several obstacles, try asking for more impulsion with leg and schooling whip. At the same time take a more positive but steady hold on the horse's mouth. This will give him something to 'lean' on to help him keep going.

If your horse takes hold and rushes his fences then devote more time to canter work on the flat. Afterwards ride over poles and obstacles on turns and circles. When jumping you can place three or even four trotting poles on the landing side to help slow him down.

5 GYMNASTIC JUMPING EXERCISES

When building up a confident partnership with your horse you might like to try some more ambitious gymnastic work.

A well-known and useful exercise is the three-fence grid which you can build with a minimum of equipment. A low regulating fence, 1ft 3ins high, is set at a 'bounce' distance from a 2ft high fence, and a slightly greater bounce distance (because of the extra height) is set to the third, 2ft, fence. The grid is shown diagrammatically in Fig. 13.

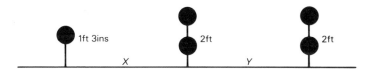

Fig. 13 *A gymnastic double.*

The distances *X* and *Y* should be made to conform to your pony/horse's height as follows:

	Distance *X*	Distance *Y*
13.2 hh	6ft	7ft 6ins
14.2 hh	6ft 6ins	8ft
15.2 hh	7ft 6ins	8ft 9ins
16.2 hh	8ft 6ins	10ft

To help a young horse lengthen when jumping, bascule-developing bars can be employed. A pole is placed 3ft 3ins from the first of two low fences and the horse has to exert a moderate degree of stretch in order to land beyond the pole. He is then expected to take off immediately, over a 2ft fence. This exercise must be used with care. If, after the horse has jumped the exercise a first time, the pole has rolled out further than the recommended distance, the horse may over-stretch himself in trying to clear it a second time. An experienced horse will take such things in his stride, but a young horse could well end up with spinal troubles as a result. When the FEI (International Equestrian Federation) talk euphemistically about an 'unpleasant surprise' for a young horse, they are probably referring to a 6ft wide parallel whose far rail is invisible to the jumping horse; but lesser 'surprises' can not only be unpleasant but downright dangerous. Whatever its level of training, never stretch your animal further than is required to meet the competition it will have to face.

The distances between the elements of this exercise can be the same as X above and a really tough problem can be set by adding another fence at distance Y. The take-off distance can be regulated by placing a pole at distance Z from the final element as shown in the figure.

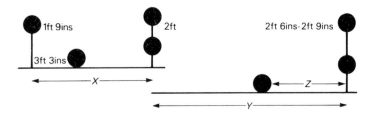

Fig. 14 *Bascule-developing bars.*

Make the distances Y and Z as follows:

	Y	Z
13.2 hh	7ft 9ins	3ft 9ins
14.2 hh	8ft 3ins	4ft
15.2 hh	9ft	4ft 3ins
16.2 hh	10ft 6ins	5ft

6 SCHOOLING OVER UPRIGHTS

Anything that keeps you off the ground sorting out fences and increases your time in the saddle is worth consideration.

When you first start jumping fences with wings it helps tremendously to put height markers on the uprights so that you know how high your fences are without having to measure them. You can, of course, achieve this with simple stripes of paint at foot heights off the ground. There is no point in making marks closer than 2ft, 3ft etc. as you can judge the intermediate heights by eye (Fig. 15).

There is one snag with using paint, for when you re-paint the fence you lose your markers. If, instead, you

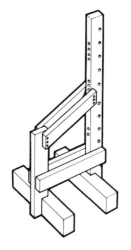

Fig. 15 *Putting height marks on your wings.*

drive groups of two, three, four, etc. galvanised roofing nails into the inside edges of your uprights you can immediately assess the fence height and the nails still show when re-painted.

Once on board the horse you will not want to dismount every few minutes in order to put back poles or adjust heights, so set three uprights side by side, all at the same height (providing you do not want to work up in height). Then you will have three fences you can knock down before you need to get off (Fig. 16).

When you feel confident of jumping the common height, grade the height of the three fences. Then if the horse knocks down the highest one you can immediately jump him over another, lower fence without a break. He will then realise that just because he knocks a pole down it does not mean he can automatically stop jumping, an impression he may gain if you stop to put back a pole every time.

Never over-face your horse by asking him too much, too soon. If he refuses show you are displeased without throwing a tantrum then try again. If he again refuses, immediately turn and jump a smaller fence. You will often find that your horse will subsequently sail over the higher jump especially if you do not allow him to wander too far before bringing him back and presenting him to the fence.

The next variation on the three-uprights theme is to set the two side fences at an angle with a cavalletto at, say, a five-stride distance (see page 110) in front of the set-up. You then ride the cavalletto and practise turning in a balanced way, and on the correct leg, into either of the angled fences. The angled fences should be uprights at first, but when you have more material you can turn them into spreads.

You will find that the horse goes better on one rein than he does on the other. Very few horses can be said

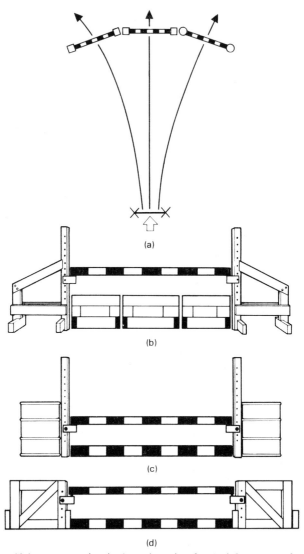

Fig. 16(a) *An exercise in jumping simple uprights examples of which are shown at* (b), (c) *and* (d).

to be equally balanced and supple on both reins and it takes a great deal of schooling to correct this. One contributory factor is that we always mount from the same (near side) and here is a good reason for practising mounting and dismounting from both sides.

It might seem a good idea to use very heavy poles or even fixed poles in order to teach an idle horse a lesson when it raps its feet on an immobile pole. With fixed rails there is no dismounting necessary because the fence will not give — only *you* will — and you may be dismounting in a rather spectacular fashion. Schooling over fixed fences is a lazy, and possibly dangerous, practice.

Hints on Riding Simple Uprights

If you do your pole and cavalletti work well, using common sense, you will reap rewards when competing. A placing pole at distance r in front of an upright will familiarise the horse with where he should take off. (Fig. 17) The distance may be shortened or lengthened slightly, but as the jump is an upright it is better approached and jumped on a short bouncy stride (you should have discovered this type of stride by doing the canter variations described on page 54).

This exercise may be improved by the quality of the trot or canter and the approach you make. Initially a wide turn will give you time and space to keep the horse 'together' and forward-going. You may find when jumping off shorter turns that the horse becomes agitated and loses balance sideways or even runs out. If, as you turn his forehand, the hindquarters swing away, he can no longer push himself forward. Thus he is not capable of 'bending' through the turn, so work him as described on pages 48 and 49.

Before you actually turn into the obstacles make sure you have impulsion not speed, so maintain a steady

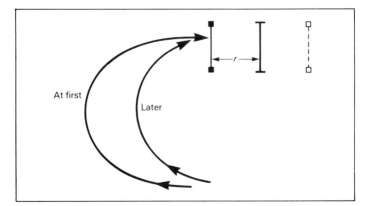

Fig. 17 *Riding into a fence off a turn. The first element is a cavalletto set at distance r from the fence. The skeletal cavalletto is a regulating one to help the horse that breaks away (r is the same as X on page 77).*

rhythm. If the horse refuses, lower the fence and ride slower, but with more leg. Use your voice to encourage the horse, but do not shout or use a high-pitched tone. The horse must never associate jumping with fear. Make turns to the left and to the right on the approach and on landing.

If you lose the horse on the turns it may be that you are pulling him round too strongly with your inside rein. This will cause the horse to 'fall' the opposite way and may even lead to a refusal. To correct this keep the inside rein steady or move it to the side (never further back or downwards), raise the outside rein and use a strong, active outside leg.

7 MEASURING YOUR HORSE'S STRIDE

Before you can judge whether a combination distance is long or short for your horse you have to know its normal stride length through combinations. In order to ascertain this you will first have to measure its stride on the flat.

Here are the standard lengths of stride on the flat for different heights of horse:

13.2 hh	14.2 hh	15.2 hh	16.2 hh
9ft	9ft 6ins	10ft 6ins	12ft

To find out if your horse strides at one of these distances choose a flat, fairly soft piece of undisturbed ground (if you can, use a raked area of an outdoor or indoor manège) and set three or four poles end to end to make a total distance of some 36ft (see Fig. 18). Ride the horse in until it has lost any initial stiffness and is going freely forward. Practise cantering past — but not over — the undisturbed ground. When you think you can do a representative run, canter over the measuring area and then come back on foot to measure the results.

When riding the horse it is the leading leg that forms the marker for each canter stride. It is not the first footfall in the canter sequence, but that does not matter. The stride is from where the leading leg strikes the ground to where it strikes the ground again. The hoof of the leading leg leaves the deepest impression and your horse's stride on the flat is the average distance over, say, three or four such footfalls.

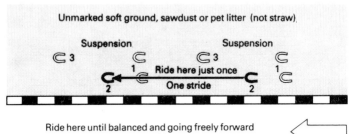

Fig. 18 *Measuring your horse's stride on the flat.*

Technically, the canter strides start as at *1*, but the stride length, S, is from the leading-leg hoof print *2* to where you find that again. Obviously you can find S just the same on the opposite rein and it can be measured from the bands on the poles.

You must now take 6 inches off the length of stride S to allow for the fact that the horse will stride that much shorter for two to three strides on landing over a fence.

You now know what one or two non-jumping strides amount to for your horse and can thus approximately measure a true distance if you add the landing distance (L) over the first fence and the take-off distance (T) over the second. The values of L and T vary with:

   (i)   the speed with which you ride the fences;
  (ii) the height of the fences;
 (iii) whether the fence is a first element or a second or a third;
 (iv) whether it is an upright, a spread or a sloping fence.

If your horse is not yet well enough schooled to take his fences at a slow, controlled pace and tends to rush them you will have to allow an extra couple of feet over the true distance, which is designed to be ridden at the slow pace recommended by the BSJA of 300yds per minute.

Take as an initial rule of thumb that you add some 3ft 6ins to the height of the first fence as a landing distance and 1ft 6ins to the height of the second fence for take-off. This is for uprights and if the fences are spreads add 2ft to the fence height for landing and keep the take-off distance the same.

Example: Your horse has a 10ft 6in. stride on the flat and so has a 10ft stride between fences of a combination. The fences are a parallel followed by an upright, both at 3ft 3ins. The true distance will be $L + S + S + T$ which in this case comes to 3ft 3ins + 2ft + (2 x 10ft) + 3ft 3ins + 1ft 6ins = 30ft. If the first fence had been an upright then the distances would have been 31ft 6ins. See Fig. 19.

Take the latter as basic and find how many of your own ordinary walking paces fit that length. You will then have a basic yardstick for combinations which you can modify by adding a little if the fences are higher and subtracting a little if they are lower. Subtract a little extra if the first fence is a spread and more again if it is a triple bar. If twelve of your own paces fit the two-stride distance then eight paces will fit a one-stride distance. However, all this is more carefully worked out in the combination section.

When you walk a combination at a show and with ordinary paces it comes to, say, thirteen and your normal yardstick is twelve then the combination is long for you. If it paces out at eleven it is short. In the first case you must encourage the horse to stretch out between the fences and in the latter you must check him in to ensure that he does not crash into the second fence.

The approach to a combination will have a definite effect on how the horse jumps it. The combination may be on a straight line and follow on closely from another fence. It is a great help then to know how many strides your horse is likely to take before he reaches the combination. If the combination comes off a fairly short turn he may over-shorten his stride on the turn. He may swing out too far which will also alter the strides. Use the exercises and suggestions given previously to help you with this.

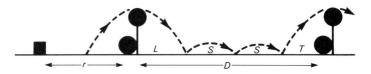

Fig. 19 *The elements of a two-stride double. L is landing distance. T is take-off distance. S is a non-jumping stride. D is the true distance between the inner faces of the fences. Distance r is that of a placing pole (see page 77).*

A True Distance Scale

Whether you are going to school a horse or a pony it is important to set the correct true distances between combinations of trotting poles and fences. You cannot be expected to carry a whole set of figures in your head so make a true distance scale as close to your schooling area as possible. This can be marked with paint on the side of the stables or a barn, or could be set out along a fence with white stakes driven into the ground at the appropriate distances. The first marks are for poles set at trotting (T) or cantering (C) distances for 13.2 hh ponies (P) or 15.2 hh horses (H). So TH is the trotting pole distance for a horse, which coincides with the cantering distance for a pony, CP.

Fig. 20 *Laying out a true distance scale.*

These distances will vary with your degree of advancement — you will want to vary them either way as the horse/pony becomes more agile — but the distances can be paced out along the scale before you set out the exercises in the schooling area.

The four basic distances you require for combinations are one and two strides for ponies and horses and the distances shown are for a combination that is, in case of the pony, 2ft 9ins high, and, for the horse, 3ft. These distances will vary with the height of fences and the height of the horse. They will alter, too, depending on whether both elements are uprights, spreads or sloping fences or a combination of these. However, the adjustments will not be great and the distance scale provides a good basis from which to work.

On the scale shown: *1P* = one stride distance for ponies; *1H* = one stride for horses; *2P* = two strides for ponies; *2H* = two strides for horses.

A scale like this is not only useful when setting up practice combinations at home, but also helps to fix the distances in your mind before going to a show and walking the course.

A true distance for a horse will be too great for a pony and vice versa so you need a guide as to the distances that should be marked for the size of mounts that you possess. The following table provides the necessary details, but if you want to lay out distances for jumping greater or lesser heights than the ones given then you must add or subtract from the figures as appropriate (see the tables of true distances in the section on combinations).

Height of pony/horse	Fence height	Two uprights	
		One stride	Two strides
12.2 hh	2ft 3ins	17ft	25ft
13.2 hh	2ft 6ins	18ft	26ft
14.2 hh	2ft 9ins	20ft	29ft
15.2 hh	3ft 0ins	21ft	31ft
16.2 hh	3ft 3ins	23ft	33ft

Height of pony/horse	Fence height	Spread followed by upright	
		One stride	Two strides
12.2 hh	2ft 3ins	16ft	23ft
13.2 hh	2ft 6ins	17ft	24ft
14.2 hh	2ft 9ins	19ft	27ft
15.2 hh	3ft 0ins	20ft	29ft
16.2 hh	3ft 3ins	22ft	31ft

Notes:
Take a foot per stride off the basic upright figures when the first element of your combination is a spread.

All distances are to be measured from the inside faces of the jumps.

The above distances are shorter than those given later in the section dealing with setting out combinations; this is because the young horse will stride short compared to his form when better schooled.

How to Set Out the Distances
You probably do not own a surveyor's tape and even if

you do it would be a chore to use such a thing. The most useful measuring device you can have is a set of poles marked in foot lengths. Lay them end to end as shown in Fig. 20 (p. 67) and mark off the appropriate distances with paint on a wall (or with hefty pegs driven in at the correct distances from a marker such as a gatepost). Fig. 20 shows four 9ft poles laid end to end giving a total length of 36ft which is more than enough for your purposes. Obviously three 12ft poles would serve equally well.

The practical advantage of having poles painted is clearly illustrated. Having used the poles for measuring they can then be utilised in your fences.

8 STARTING ON COMBINATIONS

Having started to jump single fences the next step is to set out and ride simple combinations. Here it is important that the true distance is set in the combination and without calculations this is not easy to get right. In the following section — Part Two — 'true' values are given for combinations with one or two non-jumping strides between, allowing for the different striding of ponies and horses of varying height. When fences are 'mixed', i.e. uprights, spreads or sloping, the true distances are different but not greatly so.

At first make the combination as easy as possible with set-forward groundline poles just ahead of each upright. You should have measured your horse's stride already (page 64) and so know whether the distances quoted are short or long for your particular mount. If your horse does not use himself and does not jump out of his stride then you must work on his flatwork to get him going more freely onto his bit. Hints on this are given opposite.

Suggestions for Exercises
(a) Start low and work up; practise keeping the impulsion in the non-jumping strides.
(b) Approach the combination first straight and then off turns on either rein.
(c) Re-make the fences as absolute uprights (no set-forward groundlines) and repeat previous exercises.
(CAUTION: Do not over-do the sessions. Vary the work so that the horse does not get bored. If you get con-

sistently bad results abandon the lesson and change to a hack or some other form of schooling.)

Coping with Jumping Problems

Refusing: A common fault which can lead to refusals at fences is the rider dropping the rein contact immediately in front of a jump. A young or unbalanced horse will fall onto his forehand and therefore find it difficult to lift himself over the fence. The horse which is inattentive to his rider's leg is likely to refuse whenever he is worried. The answer to this is more flatwork. Sharpen the horse's responses by making frequent transitions and changes within the pace; change direction often; and make circles of various sizes.

A horse may refuse at the first part of a combination because he is unsure of the amount of space between the fences. To overcome this build two uprights and ride figure-of-eight shapes first in trot, then in canter. Jump the second part of the combination through the figure-of-eight shape. Once the horse is going fluently and with confidence put the two jumps together, jump off both reins in both directions.

Running out: This can be difficult to cure particularly for an inexperienced rider. First, try to work out if the horse runs out always to one side or to both. The word 'runs' should give you a hint here. It means the horse has increased his speed and dropped his weight towards one shoulder. Once he has done this he cannot stop himself, and the rider cannot stop him either. If the horse runs out to the left you must 'block' the horse's left movement *before* it occurs. A horse with a tendency to run out to the left will probably jump easier off the left rein. Approach the jump slowly with a good contact, especially on the left side, and positive leg aids. Carry your whip on the left. If he still attempts to run out use the whip sharply down the left side of his neck and make him halt as soon as you can. Turn away to the right and re-establish the horse on the left rein.

When jumping off the right rein on a horse which runs out to the left, keep a good contact and when turning into the jump raise the left rein and open the right one to the side. Use active leg aids, but do not allow the horse to increase speed.

Competition Notes

Since it is likely that you will be trying to gain experience in local competitions at this stage, the following notes are given to help you make the most of the event:

(1) Walk the course. Walk the exact track you intend to ride.

(2) Stride out any short distances between fences and in combinations.

(3) Know how much time it takes to work your horse in and try to coincide this with when you are likely to enter the ring.

(4) Know how many jumps are away from the ring entrance.

(5) Do not stand about in the collecting area so as to tire and bore the horse.

(6) When in the ring concentrate on how well the horse goes between the fences.

(7) Look at each jump well before you approach it.

PART TWO

BUILDING AND RIDING FENCES IN COMBINATIONS

9 TWO UPRIGHTS

The upright fence is the configuration by which all other fences are judged so that when we consider spread fences we will always quote their heights and attributes compared to an equivalent upright fence.

The combination consisting of two uprights will be used a great deal in basic schooling for several reasons:

(1) An upright fence is the easiest to construct and uses a small amount of material. It is therefore likely that you will be able to build two uprights from a limited stock of fence material.

(2) Easy to change the height.

(3) Simple to move as there are only two pairs of wings.

(4) The combination can be ridden both ways without danger. Spread fences must usually only be ridden in the correct direction.

(5) A horse can jump an upright off his hocks if he needs to get out of trouble after arriving at the fence. He may not be able to clear a spread fence from standing.

(6) There are probably more ways of making upright fences than any other shape.

(7) When first learning to build courses for yourself you are less likely to make many mistakes with upright fences.

When learning to ride combinations you will almost certainly use speed to overcome the problem of not having enough impulsion. This means that you will land a relatively long way from the first fence. The horse will then shorten his stride from its normal value when riding on the flat, for two to three strides after landing. As combinations can only have one or two strides in them (a three-stride combination becomes a related distance) so this shortening has to be taken into account when calculating the true distance between the fences.

Despite the shortening the second fence will be jumped short, i.e. at a closer range than the correctly ridden first fence. When you become experienced and your horse well-schooled you will emulate the advanced showjumpers and ride both fences by placing your horse relatively close to each element in turn. This only becomes important when you cross the '4 foot divide' that separates the fence heights that most horses can jump without much help from their riders from those where precision of placing becomes essential (Fig. 21).

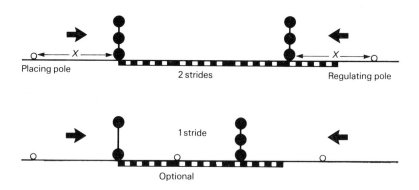

Fig. 21 *Setting out a combination of two uprights with either a two- or one-stride distance between them. Three or four 9ft poles are being used here.*

You can begin to work towards arriving at the fences at the correct point by using a placing pole set at a distance X from the first fence. This pole is placed about seven big (human) strides out from the fence when dealing with big horses, i.e. 16.2 hh, but X must obviously be less than this for smaller horses and ponies, as follows:

13.2 hh	14.2 hh	15.2 hh	16.2 hh
17ft	18ft	19ft 6ins	21ft

A common fault with fresh horses and ponies is that of charging off, a problem which many riders fail to correct in the euphoria of having cleared the fences. To help counter this, place a low regulating cavelletto or similar at the same distance (X) from the second fence of the combination. This will then make the combination symmetrical both ways and act as a placing pole when ridden in the opposite direction.

Another useful placing pole is illustrated in the one-stride combination in Fig. 21. Set as shown it produces a better length of stride between the elements from animals whose stride is less forward-going than it should be for their size. Having taught your horse or pony to stretch between the elements this pole can be dispensed with.

You can use your own paces, measured from the true-distance scale on page 68, for setting out the distances between the fences, but as will be seen from the table below the basic lengths (given in feet) need modifying for size of mount and height of fences. Errors of half a foot either way should not be important.

	12.2 hh		13.2 hh		14.2 hh	
Fence height	1 stride	2 strides	1 stride	2 strides	1 stride	2 strides
2ft 3ins	17½	25	18½	26½	19½	28½
2ft 9ins	18½	26	19½	28	20½	30½
3ft 3ins	20	27½	21	29½	21½	31½
3ft 9ins	20½	28	21½	30	22½	32
4ft 3ins	21½	29	22½	31	23½	33

	15.2 hh		16.2 hh	
Fence height	1 stride	2 strides	1 stride	2 strides
2ft 3ins	20½	30½	22	31½
2ft 9ins	22	32½	23½	33½
3ft 3ins	23	33½	24½	34½
3ft 9ins	23½	34	25	35
4ft 3ins	24	35	25½	36

The distances given will need to be shortened with novice animals who are not yet going forward properly. In any event shortening them by half a foot for a one-stride and a foot for a two-stride distance is good experience at any stage of training.

Figures 22(a) — (l) show a few different kinds of upright that can be built. They can also be used for the leading elements of other fences.

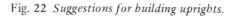

Fig. 22 *Suggestions for building uprights.*

(a) *Simple, low, schooling cross-poles. The novice horse can be helped if a groundline pole is laid along the bottom.*

(b) *The above quickly transforms into a simple upright.*

(c) *A rather more formidable but easily constructed true upright. Solidity is reinforced if a groundline pole is used.*

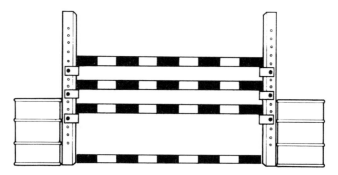

(d) *The classic upright of poles – badly put together with a big gap.*

(e) *Brush boxes filled with conifer or broom (for example) make excellent fence fillers. Left to the elements they lose their looks rapidly.*

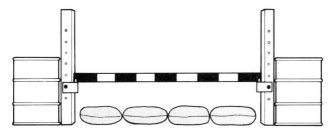

(f) *A cheap filler is provided by plastic (or even paper) sacks stuffed with old straw or hay.*

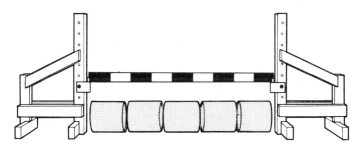

(g) *Cans placed as shown are dangerous because a refusing horse could roll them and possibly stumble over them. Instead put poles either side as illustrated on page 85, or stand the cans upright.*

(h) *Cross-poles require accurate jumping. This fence should be jumped from the far side or the horizontal pole cannot fall.*

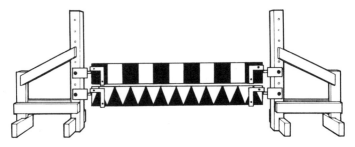

(i) *Planks are the downfall of careless jumpers and it is essential to practise over them. Buy them ready-made or make them as shown on page 159.*

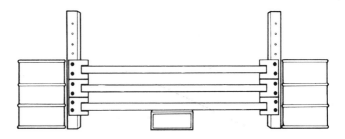

(j) *A stile will catch out even more careless combinations of horse and rider than will planks. Easy to make, as shown on page 157.*

(k) *Ringing the changes on the cross-poles theme. This should be jumped from the side shown and as depicted is a coursebuilder's friend after a tight turn on the right rein.*

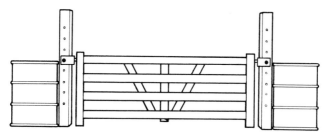

(l) *A gate is another fence that catches the unwary. Either scour local farms or buy the pig-pen kind as shown here.*

10 SLOPING FENCE AND UPRIGHT

When built large this combination should be set up as shown in Fig. 23 with the spread fence as the first element. The table on page 86 gives the true distances through this form of combination but when the first element is a triple bar 6ins should be added to the distances.

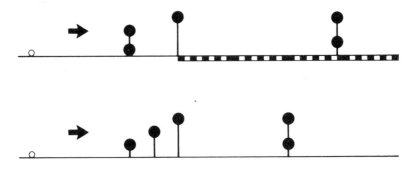

Fig. 23 *Examples of combinations utilising a sloping fence followed by an upright.*

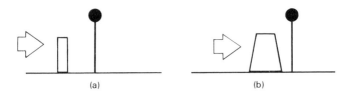

Fig. 24 *Ideas for sloping fences.* (a) *A hurdle and a pole.* (b) *A box and a pole.*

(c) *Ascending parallel with a facilitating filler.*
(d) *Ascending parallel with brush boxes or other filler. Note groundline pole.*

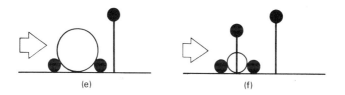

(e) *Barrel plus a pole. Ground poles prevent barrel rolling.*
(f) *Ascending parallel with cans as a filler.*

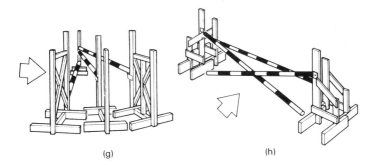

(g) *Build a radial ascending fence for a curve.*
(h) *Example of an ascending cross-pole fence.*

	12.2 hh		13.2 hh		14.2 hh	
Fence height	1 stride	2 strides	1 stride	2 strides	1 stride	2 strides
2ft 3ins	17	24½	18	26½	19	28½
2ft 9ins	18	25½	19	27½	20	29½
3ft 3ins	19	26½	20	28½	21	30½
3ft 9ins	19½	27	20½	29	21½	31
4ft 3ins	20	27½	21	29½	22	31½

	15.2 hh		16.2 hh	
Fence height	1 stride	2 strides	1 stride	2 strides
2ft 3ins	20	30½	21	32½
2ft 9ins	21	31½	22	33½
3ft 3ins	22	32½	23	34½
3ft 9ins	22½	33	23½	35
4ft 3ins	23	33½	24	35½

11 BUILDING SPREAD FENCES

When you build spread fences there are certain do's and don'ts. One don't is imperative as it is highly dangerous: *there must never be more than a single pole on any trailing element of a spread fence*. The reason is simple. A horse that lands short runs the risk of getting its hindlegs scissored in the poles and breaking a leg.

So whenever spread fences are built into your training courses at home you must always devise courses which bring you into spreads from the same direction. This will become evident in the course-plan section.

When fillers are used to make a spread appear more solid — which is a very good idea — ensure that there is a true groundline under the leading part of the fence or even facilitate jumping by using a set-forward ground-line. This should be a pole laid on the ground in the case of an ascending parallel. If you use a cavalletto or similar you have turned an ascending parallel into a triple bar.

In essence the triple bar is an ascending parallel with a slightly raised groundline ahead of it. The horse will tend to measure his take-off from the first element of the ascending parallel and so will take off close to the groundline.

If the spread is S feet then the real height of a true parallel is greater by 1½ins per foot of spread. So a fence built with elements at 3ft and a spread of 2ft becomes in effect a fence of 3ft 3ins.

In the case of an ascending parallel or a triple bar the spread coefficient c has to be added to the average height of the two main elements. In the case of an

Right

Never jump this way

This must not be jumped from either direction

Fig. 25 *How not to jump spread fences.*

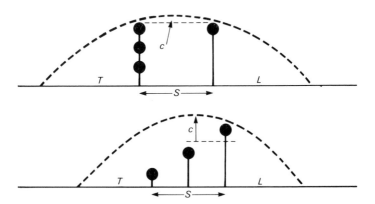

Fig. 26 *Examples of how the spread coefficient c is used to obtain the true height of a spread. To ensure that the horse does not hit either leading or trailing elements of a spread, it has to jump larger than might appear from the height of the elements.*

ascending parallel with leading and trailing elements at 2ft 6ins and 3ft and a spread of 3ft we would have to add c (3 × 1½ = 4½ins) to the average height of 2ft 9ins. The effective height is therefore 3ft 1½ins.

With ascending parallels which are not built very large it is evident that the spread coefficient will not make much difference to the effective height, but with true parallels the extra height becomes significant. Thus you should always build a true parallel a hole down from the height you want, i.e. both elements at 2ft 6ins will, in effect, be a 2ft 9ins fence.

In the case of the triple bar, the spread S is the whole

spread including the groundline and here it is easy to get a total spread S of, say, 4ft which will make an extra 6 inches to be added as a spread coefficient. If there is a 6 inch difference in height between the main elements this will effectively make the fence 3 inches higher than the highest (trailing) pole.

Dimensions of Triple Bars

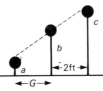

Fig. 27 *Dimensions of an ascending parallel. G is the groundline distance and for simplicity the spread between the main elements is set at 2ft.*

Desired height of fence	a	b	c	G
2ft 6ins	1ft	1ft 9ins	2ft 3ins	1ft 6ins
2ft 9ins	1ft	2ft	2ft 6ins	1ft 9ins
3ft	1ft	2ft 3ins	3ft	1ft 6ins
3ft 3ins	1ft 3ins	2ft 6ins	3ft 3ins	1ft 6ins
3ft 6ins	1ft 6ins	2ft 9ins	3ft 3ins	2ft
3ft 9ins	1ft 6ins	3ft	3ft 6ins	2ft
4ft	1ft 6ins	3ft	4ft	2ft
4ft 3ins	1ft 6ins	3ft 3ins	4ft 3ins	2ft 6ins
4ft 6ins	2ft	3ft 6ins	4ft 6ins	2ft

The above dimensions produce an easy-to-jump triple bar. If you wish to make it more difficult for the horse then lower b so that it is in the line of a to c, but do not lower it too far below this line.

Dimensions of Ascending Parallels

For reasons already given the ascending parallel induces a higher jump than would appear from its bare dimensions. Here are some suggestions for the heights *a* and *b* of the leading and trailing elements plus the width of spread *w* which will result in an effective height of given value.

Fig. 28 *Dimensions of an ascending parallel.*

Desired height of fence	a	b	w
2ft 3ins	1ft 9ins	2ft 3ins	2ft
2ft 6ins	1ft 9ins	2ft 6ins	2ft 6ins
2ft 9ins	2ft	2ft 9ins	3ft
3ft	2ft 3ins	3ft	3ft
3ft 3ins	2ft 6ins	3ft	3ft 6ins
3ft 6ins	2ft 9ins	3ft 3ins	4ft
3ft 9ins	3ft	3ft 6ins	4ft
4ft	3ft	3ft 9ins	4ft
4ft 3ins	3ft 3ins	4ft	5ft
4ft 6ins	3ft 3ins	4ft 6ins	5ft

12 UPRIGHT FOLLOWED BY A SLOPING FENCE

While it is possible to construct a true parallel which is safe to jump both ways the sloping fence only makes sense when jumped the correct way however it is constructed. In terms of material this type of combination is therefore not an economical inclusion in a home-built course.

The set-up in Fig. 29 (a) demands a considerable amount of impulsion and athleticism in the horse and, to begin with, it would be wise to drop the trailing pole of the triple bar in order to concentrate on obtaining a full-length stride between the fences. Once you are satisfied that the horse is arriving at the second element with energy, then the third pole can be added. Short-striding animals can be induced to stretch by laying a pole centrally between the fences.

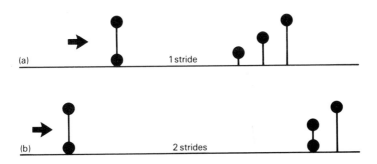

Fig. 29 *Examples of a combination consisting of* (a) *an upright followed at a one-stride distance by a triple bar, and* (b) *an upright followed at a two-stride distance by an ascending parallel.*

The set-up in Fig. 29 (b) is much more the configuration to start on and a placing pole set ahead of the upright at the distances given on page 77 will, in any case, aid the establishment of a free-flowing negotiation of

	12.2 hh		13.2 hh		14.2 hh	
Fence height	1 stride	2 strides	1 stride	2 strides	1 stride	2 strides
2ft 3ins	17	24½	18	26½	1º	28½
2ft 9ins	18	25½	19	27½	20	29½
3ft 3ins	19	26½	19½	28½	20½	30½
3ft 9ins	19½	27	20	29	21	31
4ft 3ins	20½	28	21	30	22	32

	15.2 hh		16.2 hh	
Fence height	1 stride	2 strides	1 stride	2 strides
2ft 3ins	20	30	21	32½
2ft 9ins	21	31	22	33½
3ft 3ins	21½	32	22½	34½
3ft 9ins	22	32½	23	35
4ft 3ins	23	33½	24½	35½

the combination by ensuring that the horse arrives at the first element correctly.

The rider will, especially in the early stages when not sure of the horse's ability to clear this form of combination, probably use too much speed and the young horse, or the less well-schooled horse, may charge off. This is especially so after landing over a triple bar, and a regulating cavalletto can be used to help eliminate this fault.

It may well be a coursebuilder's ploy to place another fence at a related distance beyond a combination and this set-up should also be built when you have the material and the room. The related distance should start perhaps with five strides and gradually be reduced to three. A bend to one side or the other can be allowed in the related distance but it will be well to follow the spread by an upright — and lack of material will often lead to this correct result.

The distances in the table opposite are a little shorter than when the order of spread and upright is reversed, and shorter than with a simple pair of uprights. They are for an ascending parallel as second element and can be shortened by half a foot per stride when alternatively a triple bar is built.

13 TRUE PARALLEL AND UPRIGHT

A true parallel or oxer can be made into the most formidable fence on any course. It needs to look solid but should never be made over-square, i.e. never wider than it is high. In early stages of training and especially with young horses without sufficient strength in their backs, asking for a stretch over a wide parallel is likely to lead to trouble. This may not show itself at first but later 'cold back' or other evidence of spinal trouble may develop. So start off relatively narrow and only later, after athletic exercises have strengthened the back muscles, expect your horse to jump a wide parallel.

Make sure that whatever fillers are used to solidify the appearance of the fence do not obstruct the horse's

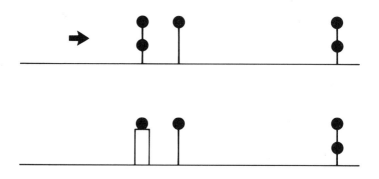

Fig. 30 *Examples of a combination consisting of a true parallel followed by an upright.*

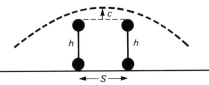

Fig. 31 *Calculating the spread coefficient.*

view of the trailing pole. This can happen when brush-boxes are used.

The leading and trailing elements of a true parallel must as a rule be 3–6 inches lower than the desired height of the fence. This is because of the spread coefficient c. As this is 1½ inches per foot of spread, so a 2ft wide spread S makes the effective height (b + 3ins). The value $c = 6$ins only truly belongs to advanced jumping where the height and spread have increased to around 4ft.

	12.2 hh		13.2 hh		14.2 hh	
Fence height	1 stride	2 strides	1 stride	2 strides	1 stride	2 strides
2ft 3ins	17	24½	18	26½	19	28½
2ft 9ins	18½	26	19½	28	20½	30
3ft 3ins	19½	27	20½	29	21½	31
3ft 9ins	20	27½	21	29½	22	31½
4ft 3ins	20½	28	21½	30	22½	32

| Fence height | 15.2 hh | | 16.2 hh | |
	1 stride	2 strides	1 stride	2 strides
2ft 3ins	20	30½	21	32½
2ft 9ins	21½	32	22½	34
3ft 3ins	22½	32½	23½	35
3ft 9ins	23	33	24	35½
4ft 3ins	23½	33½	24½	36

Because the true distances are measured between the insides of the two fences and the bascule comes to its highest point within the fence itself, so the distances in the above table are slightly less than for a pair of equivalent uprights. However, the apparent exactness of the figures must not cloud the realisation that inches either way are not going to make very much difference. In fact varying these 'true' distances, and especially making them longer as your training proceeds, is a very good thing to do. When you go to shows the chances that an absolutely 'true' distance has been set in the combinations is small. In any case what is true for one horse is not necessarily true for another.

You can build a true parallel in the normal way or you can help to facilitate the horse in negotiating it by putting in a set-forward groundline pole. A set-back or aggravated groundline is not actually considered fair for novice horses but that does not mean you will not have to meet it. See Fig. 32.

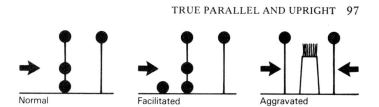

Fig. 32 *Changing the degree of difficulty of a true parallel or oxer. The normal and facilitated versions can be jumped only one way; the aggravated version can be jumped both ways.*

Below are some suggested dimensions which will result in true parallels around the desired heights. If some of these appear 'over-square' then remember that the true height is the height of the elements plus the spread coefficient.

Desired height	Height of elements	Spread
2ft 3ins	2ft	2ft
2ft 9ins	2ft 6ins	2ft
3ft 3ins	2ft 9ins	3ft
3ft 9ins	3ft 3ins	4ft
4ft 3ins	3ft 9ins	4ft

Some ideas on how to ring the changes on the theme of the true parallel are shown in Fig. 33.

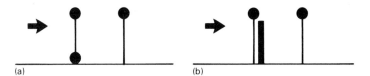

Fig. 33 *Ideas for true parallels and oxers.*
(a) *A low fence using three poles.*
(b) *A true parallel using two poles plus a filler.*

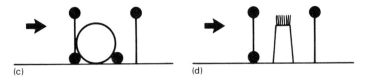

(c) (d)

(c) *Four poles plus barrels as a filler; note that poles will prevent the barrels rolling.*

(d) *Three-pole oxer plus brush-box filler. Only when there is brush in the middle is a parallel truly an oxer. Put in a groundline pole for novices.*

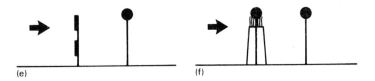

(e) (f)

(e) *Planks and rail. Use planks for the leading plane of the parallel but never anything but a pole in the trailing plane.*

(f) *Two poles plus brush-box filler in leading plane — a very solid fence.*

14 UPRIGHT FOLLOWED BY A TRUE PARALLEL

This is quite a formidable combination especially if built with a one-stride distance. It should be kept low to start with and only with time, when both horse and rider have developed muscle and confidence, should it be built up.

In Fig. 34 (a) a two-stride distance has an upright of planks or a gate followed by a parallel with only one pole on each upright but with a substantial filler under the leading pole. This can be jumped only one way.

Fig. 34 *Examples of a combination consisting of an upright followed by a true parallel.*

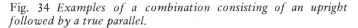

(a)

(a) *Because of the way the parallel is built it should be jumped only in direction shown.*

(b)

(b) *Build a symmetrical oxer and the combination can be jumped either way.*

In the case of Fig. 34 (b) a simple upright is followed by a one-stride distance and an oxer with a set-back groundline makes an advanced form of combination.

However, because of the symmetry of the oxer it may be jumped both ways.

	12.2 hh		13.2 hh		14.2 hh	
Fence height	1 stride	2 strides	1 stride	2 strides	1 stride	2 strides
2ft 3ins	17½	25	18½	27	19½	29
2ft 9ins	18½	26	19½	28	20½	30
3ft 3ins	19½	27	20½	29	21½	31
3ft 9ins	20½	28	21½	30	22½	32
4ft 3ins	21	28½	22	30½	23	32½

	15.2 hh		16.2 hh	
Fence height	1 stride	2 strides	1 stride	2 strides
2ft 3ins	20½	31	21½	33
2ft 9ins	21½	32	22½	34
3ft 3ins	22½	33	23½	35
3ft 9ins	23½	34	24½	35½
4ft 3ins	24	34½	25	36

15 SLOPING FENCE FOLLOWED BY A TRUE PARALLEL

Sloping fences encourage a horse to jump large and boldly so the landing distance beyond a triple bar is also larger than with true parallels or even sloping parallels. The table overleaf is for a combination as shown in Fig. 35 where the first element is a triple bar. If an ascending parallel is built as the first element then take a foot off two-stride distances and 6 inches off one-stride distances.

The arrangement of sloping fence followed by a true parallel may be more demanding than when the order is reversed, and the horse must be really forward-going before this sequence is attempted. Even then the true parallel should be built low (whatever you intend to build the triple bar or ascending parallel to) and invitingly because it is very easy for the unmuscled horse to lose impulsion and so refuse or run out at the apparently formidable true parallel.

You, the rider, must also be confident of your ability to ride other lesser combinations because unless you are certain in your own mind that you can ride smoothly and with maintained impulsion through a difficult combination such as this, it would be better not to attempt it.

Fig. 35 *Example of a combination consisting of a sloping fence followed by a true parallel.*

	12.2 hh		13.2 hh		14.2 hh	
Fence height	1 stride	2 strides	1 stride	2 strides	1 stride	2 strides
2ft 3ins	17	24½	18	26½	19	28½
2ft 9ins	18	25½	19	27½	20	29½
3ft 3ins	18½	26	19½	28	20½	30
3ft 9ins	19	26½	20	28½	21	30½
4ft 3ins	19½	27	20½	29	21½	31

	15.2 hh		16.2 hh	
Fence height	1 stride	2 strides	1 stride	2 strides
2ft 3ins	20	30½	21	32½
2ft 9ins	21	31½	22	33½
3ft 3ins	21½	32	22½	34
3ft 9ins	22	32½	23	34½
4ft 3ins	22½	33	23½	35

At home, with a comparatively small amount of material, it may not be possible to build two spread fences anyway as it requires at least four pairs of wings and some form of stands to take the groundline pole of the triple bar. This may leave nothing over for any other fences elsewhere. Thus such combinations will often be ridden in isolation. This is perfectly acceptable, but approaches on either rein should be attempted so that you can practice lining up correctly for the first fence. As mentioned elsewhere you can jump uprights at an angle, but spread fences must be attacked directly.

16 TRUE PARALLEL FOLLOWED BY A SLOPING FENCE

This combination will produce the shortest true distances because the bascule over the true parallel should come to its zenith within the spread of the fence and so the horse will land a relatively short distance from the trailing pole. The sloping character of a triple bar, and to a lesser extent an ascending parallel, makes for a close take-off and therefore both landing and take-off distances are relatively short.

This arrangement is less demanding of the horse than the one where the true parallel is the second element but remarks made under that heading also apply to this form of double-spread combination.

	12.2 hh		13.2 hh		14.2 hh	
Fence height	1 stride	2 strides	1 stride	2 strides	1 stride	2 strides
2ft 3ins	16½	26	17½	26	18½	28
2ft 9ins	17½	25	18½	27	19½	29
3ft 3ins	18½	26	19½	28	20½	30
3ft 9ins	19	26½	20	28½	21	30½
4ft 3ins	19½	27	20½	29	21½	31

	15.2 hh		16.2 hh	
Fence height	1 stride	2 strides	1 stride	2 strides
2ft 3ins	19½	30	20½	32
2ft 9ins	20½	31	21½	33
3ft 3ins	21½	32	22½	34
3ft 9ins	22	32½	23	34½
4ft 3ins	22½	33	23½	35

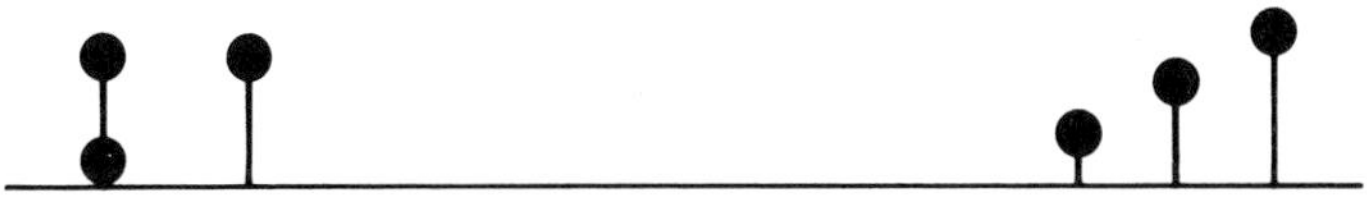

Fig. 36 *Example of a combination consisting of a true parallel followed by a sloping fence.*

17 MAKING A COMBINATION MORE DIFFICULT

Starting with a simple pair of uprights you can proceed to make a combination more and more demanding for yourself and your horse. The principles involved include:

(i) One-stride combinations are more demanding than two-stride set-ups.

(ii) Putting a true parallel first makes for tougher jumping than putting a sloping fence first.

(iii) Because of the effort involved a spread fence that follows an upright is more demanding than the other way round. Ponies should not be asked to jump such combinations when the heights are the maximum for their stage of training.

(iv) The use of light planks to catch out a sloppy jumper.

Thus Fig. 37 (a) to (k) shows:

(a) The basic two-stride upright combination which will generally be the first combination a horse is asked to jump.

(b) The first fence is made into an easy ascending parallel which is well filled to encourage the horse to respect it.

(c) The ascending parallel is made into a true parallel.

(d) While a triple-bar is assumed to be easier to jump than other spread fences it may not appear so to the novice because of its apparently greater spread.

(e) Reversing the order so that the spread fence comes second makes a more difficult combination as novices easily run out of steam between the fences. Further, the effort of negotiating the first fence and the subsequent loss of balance can make jumping

Fig. 37(a)–(k) *Combinations — progressive degrees of difficulty.*

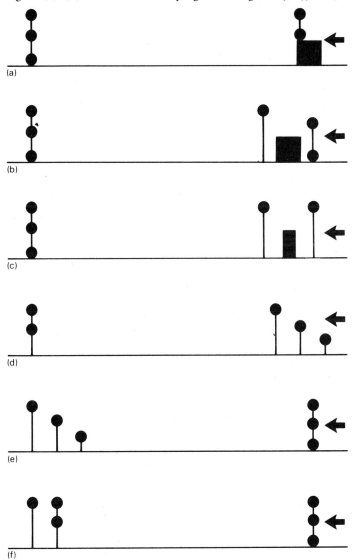

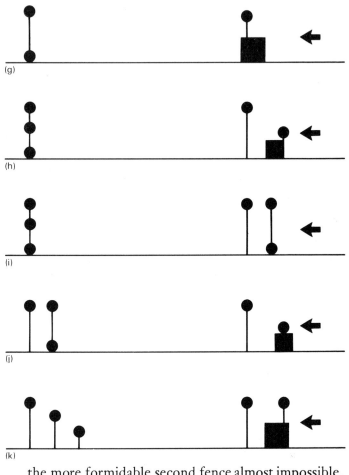

(g)

(h)

(i)

(j)

(k)

the more formidable second fence almost impossible. In early attempts at this combination keep the spread fence low.

(f) The true parallel following the upright should not be asked of ponies. It may be as well to keep horses away from it also until they have developed considerable jumping muscle.

(g) All the above can be made more difficult and demanding of horse and rider by shortening the distance to a one-stride length.

(h) Increasing the spread together with the one-stride distance makes for a considerable increase in difficulty.

(i) The formidable true parallel with an upright to follow should be increased in height slowly and work stopped before the horse has reached its maximum effort.

(j) Spread-to-spread combinations will vary in difficulty depending on whether the sloping fence is placed first, or

(k) placed after the true parallel (in which case it is easier).

The difficulty and demands can be increased by:

(1) Building two true parallels at either one- or two-stride distances.

(2) Increasing height and/or spread of either or both, but especially the second.

(3) Building any form of treble with either two-strides or one-stride in both parts. Try a combination followed by a related distance first (page 110).

(4) Building trebles with parallels especially as the intermediate or final fence of the three.

(5) Building two strides into the first part and one stride into the second or vice versa.

All these alternatives are for the well-developed, well-muscled animal with a rider who possesses skill and confidence. They are not for the young horse nor for the novice rider. If you demand this kind of effort from all but the most athletic ponies you may be asking for trouble.

18 PACING RELATED AND COMBINATION DISTANCES

It is generally assumed that any number of strides between three and seven occurring between following fences is a related distance. The horse will shorten its stride for a couple of paces after landing as it absorbs its own momentum, but then the stride will lengthen to the normal value. The following table is a guide to the related distances to set for three, four or five paces between the fences for pony and horse heights of 13.2 hh and above. Small ponies can sort their feet out so cleverly that setting correct distances for them is largely unnecessary and the 13.2 values can be used here.

	13.2 hh			14.2 hh			15.2 hh			16.2 hh		
Fence height	strides 3 4 5			strides 3 4 5			strides 3 4 5			strides 3 4 5		
2ft 3ins	feet 35 44 53			feet 37 46 56			feet 40 50 61			feet 43 54 65		
2ft 9ins	36 45 54			38 47 57			41 51 62			44 55 66		
3ft 3ins	37 46 55			39 48 58			42 52 63			45 56 67		
3ft 9ins	38 47 56			40 49 59			43 53 64			46 57 68		
4ft 3ins	39 48 57			41 50 60			44 54 65			47 58 69		

In mixed combinations these distances can be reduced as follows:

parallel to upright	
upright to parallel	all reduced by 6ins per stride
sloping to parallel	
parallel to sloping	reduced by 1ft per stride
upright to sloping	both reduced by
parallel to triple bar	1ft 6ins per stride
triple bar to parallel	distances as in table above

The distances for six and seven strides can be deduced from the intervals between the other figures, e.g. 53—44 = 9ft interval. So six strides = 62ft, and seven strides = 71ft. As these distances cannot for practical reasons be measured using poles they will have to be paced. It is often assumed that the stride of a person is somewhere about 3ft, but this is by no means so. Unless you stretch your normal stride to rather ridiculous proportions it will not be anything like 3ft. For example, I am 5ft 8ins and my normal stride is 2ft 6ins. My daughter, who is 5ft 6ins, has a normal stride of 2ft 3ins, but my wife, who is 5ft 7ins, strides as I do.

This means that twenty of my normal paces measure 50ft, whereas over the same distance my daughter takes about twenty-two paces. Obviously children will take correspondingly shorter steps and only by setting up the true-distance scale for their size of mount and striding it out themselves can they hope to obtain a useful idea of their personal pacings.

If you do not wish to set out a true-distance scale or for some reason it is impossible, the following table will serve the same purpose.

To find your stride length, first lay two poles end to end. They may be 9ft, 10ft or 12ft long. If they are 12ft then the total distance is 24ft. Pace this out and find how many of your paces it is at normal stride. If it

Combination distance in feet

Personal stride (paces)	15	16	17	18	19	20	21	22	23	24	25	26	27	28	29	30	31	32	33	34	35	36
1ft 9ins		9		10	11		12		13		14	15		16		17		18	19		20	
2ft		8		9		10		11		12		13		14		15		16		17		18
2ft 3ins		7		8		9			10		11		12		13			14		15		16
2ft 6ins	6			7		8			9		10			11		12			13		14	
2ft 9ins			6		7			8			9			10		11			12			13
3ft	5			6			7			8			9			10			11			12

Related distance in feet

Personal stride (paces)	36	38	40	42	44	46	48	50	52	54	56	58	60	62	64	66	68	70	72	74	76	78
1ft 9ins	20	21	22	23	24	25	26	27	28	29	30	31	32	33	34	35	36	37	38	39	40	41
2ft	18	19	20	21	22	23	24	25	26	27	28	29	30	31	32	33	34	35	36	37	38	39
2ft 3ins	16	17	18	19	20	21	22	23	24	25	26	26	27	28	29	30	31	32	33	34	35	36
2ft 6ins	14	15	16	17	18	18	19	20	21	22	22	23	24	25	26	26	27	28	29	30	30	31
2ft 9ins	13	14	15	15	16	17	17	18	19	20	20	21	22	23	23	24	25	25	26	27	28	28
3ft	12	13	13	14	15	15	16	17	17	18	19	19	20	21	21	22	23	23	24	25	25	26

is about eleven paces the table shows that you have a normal stride of about 2ft 3ins. If a child takes twelve paces over the same distance the stride is 2ft. With two 9ft poles, eight paces will indicate a stride of 2ft 3ins whereas six paces means a stride of 3ft.

Once you know your stride length you can refer to the table to find the normal number of paces for, say, a 21ft distance or a 32ft distance, and so on. For example my daughter often rides our 14.2 hh Welsh cob over courses around 3ft 6ins and the true-distance table for two uprights (the basic distance) shows the true distance should be around 20–21ft for a one-stride combination and about 30ft for a two-stride one. Looking at the table we see that for her personal stride of 2ft 3ins the distances will be true when they occupy nine and a little over thirteen paces respectively.

However, you should try to assess whether your mount strides long or short (it will probably be the latter) compared to the table of normal strides on page 63. You may discover that what is true for your horse may not be assumed true by the coursebuilders.

Just as with the combination distances the table here will enable you to read off the number of your own personal paces for any related distance. For example, say you are riding a 14.2 hh pony over fences set at 3ft 3ins and you want a four-stride related distance. From the table on page 110 you find the distance required between the fences is 48ft. You have a personal stride of 2ft 9ins and so using the table here you need seventeen and a half paces.

Alternatively, you might like to set a six-stride distance between fences that are at 3ft 6ins and you are riding a 15.2 hh horse. For five strides the distance would be 63½ft (the ½ft is largely immaterial) to which 11ft has to be added making 73 or 74ft to be paced. Your personal stride is 2ft 3ins so you therefore need approximately thirty-three paces.

As well as combinations, related distances should be set in your more advanced training using the table above as a guide. Indoors,especially, most distances are going to be related unless the builder builds off the walls and thereby gives greater distances between one fence and the next. However, it is perhaps best to start in one straight line if you have the room, as shown in Fig. 38. It is a familiar ploy to follow a combination with a related distance thus making a 'long treble'. Thus first of all set three relatively low uprights at distances given on pages 78 and 110. Both these can be paced using the tables on page 112.

The impulsion required for this exercise is high and the horse must not be asked to do it cold. After an initial work-in he should be popped over several single fences before the combination and related distance is attempted. When it is obvious that the horse will ride through this set of uprights calmly and with impulsion at the height required then the first element could be made into a spread; and later the last element; but making the

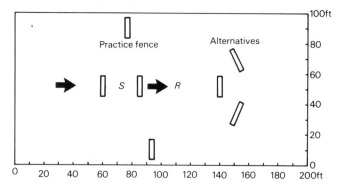

Fig. 38 *A course plan for exercises involving a combination distance S plus a related distance R leading into alternative fence positions.*

middle one a spread requires considerably more impulsion and should not be set for ponies or novice horses unless the heights are kept well within the animal's capabilities.

The related distance R shown in Fig. 38 is a four-stride distance for 15.2 hh animals at a height of about 3 ft. As an alternative you could try building a five-stride distance, but angling the approach after the combination by a small amount. If the second element of the combination is a spread this angling must be very slight and landing over it on the correct leading leg is very important as the distance in which the alteration of course has to be made is so restricted.

PART THREE

TOWARDS COURSEBUILDING

19 THE BASIC SET OF MATERIALS

You may start off by building a home jumping course with straw bales and poles balanced on cans, but if any real progress is to be made proper fences must be built. Thus you must work towards obtaining the basic minimum of equipment as outlined here:

  3 sets of wings
  6 poles — say 4 coloured and 2 rustic
  6 pairs of cups
  2 sets of fillers (straw bales, hurdles, cans etc.)
  start and finish markers

Wings may be of the usual pattern, obtained from a saddlers, or they may be ones you have made yourself from barrels or tyres etc. If you use only barrel or tyre wings they cannot be moved closer than their own diameter, which causes a problem when attempting to assemble a parallel. The wings need to be closer at first, so the more normal type is indicated. Make sure that all the uprights are drilled with holes to the same standard and that you do not buy an assortment of metric and imperial heights, otherwise you will have trouble with poles that slope if the wings get mixed.

Poles must be of a standard length. It is very useful to have them 9ft long for reasons given elsewhere, but whatever length you obtain (9ft, 10ft or 12ft) make sure you stick to that length for all your poles and, later, planks.

Cups Some ideas for making your own cups are given in the construction section, but in the end you will probably end up buying standard cups which must be the round pattern and not flat. You will be able to add flats as and when you acquire planks, gates, etc. When you get them tie the pins on very securely with strong twine as a cup without a pin is useless. Also, a pin that is trodden into the ground becomes a future potential hazard. A long bolt of the right thickness can replace a lost pin, but it is difficult to tie them to the cups and, again, you can lose these very easily.

Fillers. Sacks stuffed with straw or old fodder etc. and straw bales are fine until they begin to fall apart or sprout, so eventually you will want more permanent fillers. Here the best bet is hurdles made to a length compatible with the standard of pole-width you have adopted. If you intend to use both 12ft and 9ft poles then hurdles that are just under 3ft wide will fill both these widths. Wooden hurdles are easy to move, easy to make and take a lot of punishment.

Start and finish markers are perhaps not absolutely essential but they do add a professional touch. Empty oil or chemical cans painted red (for the right) and white (for the left) can make very serviceable markers.

What Can be Built?

With the material outlined above you can obviously build three upright fences. One can have three poles on it, but that only leaves three poles for the other two. This is where a filler (or, better still, two fillers) is essential to make up for the lack of poles and also to vary the look of the fences. Alternatively you can build a spread and an upright and make up practice combinations possibly using wooden or concrete cavalletti to simulate other fences and so give the necessary practice in riding the inevitable turns between one fence and the next. Of course you can always supplement this basic material with a bale fence (see pages 24–26). However, if you build only uprights at first and jump them both ways, quite complex courses can be ridden even with just three fences.

20 A THREE-FENCE ARENA

If you have only a limited amount of fence-building material you need to concentrate it in a relatively small space so whatever size of paddock you have, use only a small area for jumping. Among other advantages this arrangement ensures that if an area gets badly cut-up you can move elsewhere.

The size need not be greater than 150ft x 80ft, but if you have a big horse with a long stride you might find it better to settle for, say, 200ft x 160ft. A small area helps you think about what you are doing at all times rather than meandering vaguely around a larger ill-defined space. The dimensions of the area you choose are not at all critical, but it would be better to have it reasonably oblong.

Mark out your arena with white-painted building blocks (as described on page 36) and try to put old poles or other timber etc. along the sides. This will help you to conform to the confines of the arena and not fall into the habit of riding outside the allotted area. This way you will have to concentrate more on controlling the horse and also on getting him on the correct leg between fences. Your little cache of jumps will look more sensible in a small space and will teach you a great deal about riding in limited areas such as indoor schools.

To lay out the arena set a block at x (see Fig. 39) and, knowing your own personal stride length, find out the number of paces for $x - o$ for the size you intend to use. For example, you have a personal stride of 2ft 6ins and you want an arena 120ft x 150ft. You pace

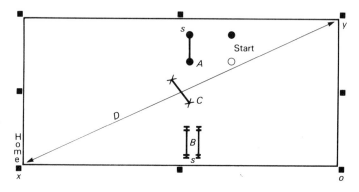

Fig. 39 *Setting out the jumping area and laying out an initial course of three fences. Course 1: A—B—A—C—B—A (B is an upright). Course 2: as (1) but with B as a parallel.*

$x - o$ with sixty of your strides and drop another block at o. Facing at right angles from $o - x$ pace forty-eight strides and place a block at y. However, if you want to make $x - o - y$ accurately square then from x pace the diagonal D with, in this case, seventy-seven paces and adjust the block at y accordingly. You can use the same idea for laying out a home schooling arena as suggested on page 45.

Setting Out the Fences

In the early stages everything must be done to encourage the horse (as well as the rider), so it is important to have the start towards the 'home' end. Even well-schooled horses do not like starting away from home and while it will be important to accustom your horse to starting the 'wrong' way, it is best to encourage him as much as possible. Home is where the horse knows he goes for food and/or freedom. It may be the entrance to the paddock, the horse's stable or the feed shed, and so you will have to use the course plans here as a guide and re-

Pacing Out the Jumping Area

$o - y$ $o - x$

Personal stride	80ft	D	100ft	120ft	D	150ft	160ft	D	200ft
1ft 9ins	Paces 46	73	57	69	110	86	91	146	114
2ft	40	64	50	60	96	75	80	128	100
2ft 3ins	36	57	44	53	85	67	71	114	88
2ft 6ins	32	51	40	48	77	60	64	102	80
2ft 9ins	29	47	36	44	70	55	58	93	73
3ft	27	43	33	40	64	50	53	85	67

orientate them with respect to whatever is 'home' for you. However, it is wise not to start a novice horse directly at 'home' or the temptation to run straight out may prove too much.

So in Fig. 39 'home' is assumed to be at the end towards which you intend to start, but is not directly ahead of the animal as he lands over the first fence. As set out, the three fences (assuming that is all you can muster) have to be supplemented by a cavalletto at C because two fences have been used to make a spread. In the early stages you can set out three uprights and maybe use the cavalletto to simulate the position of another fence.

A is a modest upright built with a set-forward ground-line; barrel wings could be used here. The groundline can be raised a little off the ground to make an approach to an ascending parallel (much loved by coursebuilders as a first fence). Try to make this fence inviting to the horse, and not in any way daunting to yourself.

One of the biggest temptations when building a course is to go for height; as soon as the horse begins to show any natural ability the fences tend to be built up too quickly. This is a sin with a young horse and especially if the landing area is hard or uneven. The fact that a willing horse will clear the jumps is no reason to flog him to death. Over-jumped horses soon go off jumping altogether and become careless and bored. If you sense that this is happening do something else. Take the animal out for a quiet hack or, if you cannot do that, reward him by returning him to his stable or by turning him out into a field or paddock.

Initially make B a simple upright and leave spaces (s) so that you can ride by. Gaps like these open up many more avenues of approach to the few fences you have. If B is an upright then C could be a cross-poles or, by pressing the cavalletto into service, it could be made into an ascending parallel with rather more spread than was earlier suggested for fence *A*.

Courses to Ride (following Fig. 39)

Course (1) A simple course with very few problems starts over *A* and then over *B* as an upright. The turn to *C* requires balance and more control than you may have with a young horse, so ride *A* again and tackle *C* along the diagonal *D* towards *y*. If a form of ascending parallel is built here it can only be jumped looking towards *y*. However, *B* can be jumped both ways and it can be jumped off the opposite rein to finish over *A* through the start.

You may have problems at first when approaching *B*; it is away from home and the horse will be disappointed that he is made to go on and so becomes sluggish and loses impulsion. If this happens get him used to the idea that he is not going to go out every time he goes near home by repeating the start sequence and then just riding him past *B* without jumping. You can then concentrate on maintaining impulsion and balance without having the worry of a fence to negotiate as well. When he seems to have settled and rides past the home corner (*x*) calmly you can then tackle fence *B* again.

A frequent problem is that on jumping *A* the horse will try to take off, and while it is all very well to say that he should not, he very often does. So place a regulating cavalletto after *A* the distance recommended on page 77. This will slow up the horse and enable you to regain control so that your approach to *B* is also steadied, but here, again, a placing cavalletto in front of *B* will help to suggest to the horse that he should slow down. Moreover it will place him correctly for the fence and make it more likely that he will jump it cleanly.

Course (2) The character of the course (a) is changed

if *B* is built as a true parallel (note the strictures about building parallels that can be jumped both ways, page 88), but the above remarks apply. Parallels must be approached straight and not jumped on the angle which in this simple course is not likely anyway.

Course (3) The relative positions of *A* and *B* can make a considerable difference to the difficulty of the approach to *B* as shown in Fig. 40. In (a) the parallel *B* is built 'downstream' of *A* and this is an easy arrangement as the turn naturally brings you straight into the parallel. In (b) you have to ride on in order to be sure of having enough space to approach the parallel correctly. You need at least three non-jumping strides (and it would be better to have more) in a straight line into the fence.

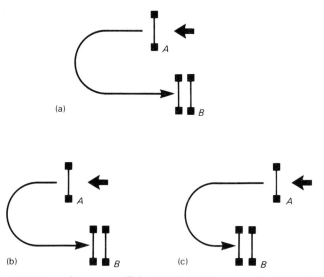

Fig. 40 *Turns into a parallel: (a) With B 'upstream' of A this is the easiest; (b) When B is opposite A you need to ride on before turning; (c) With B 'downstream' of A you need good judgment on the turn.*

With experience some of these strides could be on the turn, but even seasoned riders like to approach parallels quite straight.

The arrangement (c) is one coursebuilders like to incorporate in jump-off courses as the temptation to cut the corner is, for many, irresistible; if a rider approaches the parallel at an angle the horse either refuses, runs out or, if it jumps, hits the fence.

Knowing how far to ride on after landing over the first fence is a matter of experience, but initially it is important to give yourself more than enough approach distance when riding into the parallel. You then ride the exercise over a period of time concentrating on getting the horse on the correct leg, keeping balance and impulsion round the bend and finding by trial and error how successful you are when you cut the corner. If the fence height is well within your scope you can often get away with a too-sharp turn after A.

Fig. 41 *Courses with four or five fences laid out in areas of different size. Lay out these different-sized jumping areas using the table of paces given on page 123.*

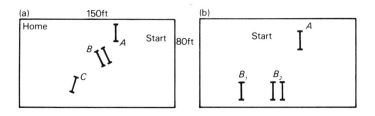

(a) *Using four pairs of wings. A and C are true uprights; B is a true parallel. Try riding A—C—A—B—C—A.*

(b) *Using four pairs of wings. $B_1 - B_2$ is a two-stride combination. Try riding A—B_2—B_1—A—B_1—B_2—A.*

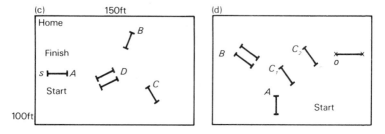

(c) *Using five pairs of wings. Try riding A–B–D, (go right) B–D, (go left) C–D–A.*

(d) *Using five pairs of wings. Try riding A–B–C$_2$–C$_1$–o–B–A–C$_2$–C$_1$.*

21 BUILDING UP YOUR HOME COURSE

By now, you have put together a basic set of materials and performed some useful exercises over the fences you have built. With the following you can build more-demanding courses:

  6 pairs of wings
12 poles
  2 planks
  3 sets of hurdles, brush boxes or other fillers
  1 set of stile cups and bars
  1 gate
12 pairs of round cups
  3 pairs of flat cups
  start and finish flags or markers

With this amount of material you can build a jump-both-ways course consisting of a round of eight or more fences which will give that essential practice in maintaining impulsion through a full series of obstacles. Such a course is shown in Fig. 42 (overleaf).

Following Fig. 42 fence (1) can be a low upright which is well filled in a vertical plane — a simple pole over straw bales or stuffed sacks would suffice.

The turn into (2) is wide and flowing and as (2) is set downstream of (1) the arrangement is wholly conducive to easy jumping. Thus (2) could be an upright of, say, three poles set a hole or possibly two higher than (1). There is then a gentle turn into (3) which can be a cross-pole as, together with the turn, this form of fence demands obedience of the horse. Do not forget that the actual height of a cross-pole fence is somewhat higher than the height of the cross. Also horses do tend to jib at the confined nature of this form of fence.

The combination (4) is going to be jumped only one way and so (4a) can be an ascending parallel made more inviting by being filled with hurdles. Barrel wings and a gate would form a good answer to (4b). Set on the diagonal of the arena as shown, there is ample room for a two-stride distance or, if preferred, two distinct fences with a three-stride length between the elements.

The 220° turn into (5) demands more care and control than did the 180° one from (1) to (2), but this fence is a low one as it is (1) jumped the other way. Care must be taken to ride into the cross-poles of fence (6) straight as there may be a temptation to cut across the fence at an angle. The effective height of such a fence increases sharply when approached diagonally.

Fences (7) and (8) should not present difficulties as

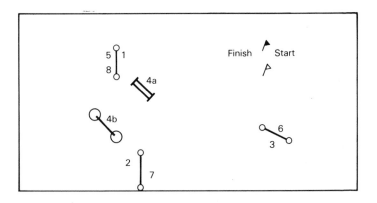

Above: Fig. 42 *A full round of eight fences utilising six pairs of wings and including a double.*
Opposite: Fig. 43 *Suggestions for fences which could be built in the course shown in Fig. 42.*

Fence 1

Fence 3

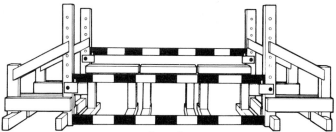

Fence 4a

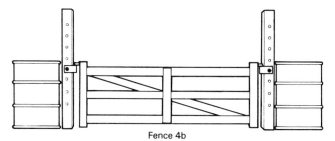

Fence 4b

they are the first two fences in the course anyway.

Jumping the same fences twice or even three times may not be ideal but the object here is to maintain impulsion and control, and accustom the horse to the idea of jumping full courses.

You can now try a jump-off course consisting of (1), (2), (4a and b) (the rules say that if there is a combination in the event there has to be one in the jump-off), (5) and (7) to finish in the bottom left-hand corner. With a digital stop-watch you can time the rounds yourself but make sure that the start and finish flags are a good distance from the first and last fences respectively so that you have time to start the watch, settle to the first fence and stop the watch when over the last fence.

Figure-of-Eight Courses

The figure-of-eight is the classic design on which many show-jumping courses are based. It provides the important (almost compulsory) change of rein, and it utilises the diagonals which, in a restricted space, is where the combinations nearly always have to be placed (Fig. 44).

It has other equally important attributes, for example it provides the largest number of alternative courses within the same set of fences or with very little shifting of fences. As well as the course shown you could swing right after (1) and take (5) which would lead into the combination the opposite way. With more fences on the ground many other alternatives will begin to appear, but to begin with, let us assume that you have material for five fences and no more. Thus (1) and (2) will have to be simulated fences using cavalletti or similar because this course includes a combination (3a and b) and a related distance of five strides from (5) to (6) on the diagonals.

In designing such a course you simply have to sketch a rather squashed figure of eight and set your fences on

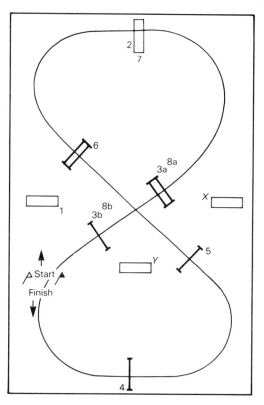

Fig. 44 *A basic figure-of-eight course plan with alternative placings (see text).*

it knowing that your turns and approaches are bound to be flowing and would cause very few to complain.

Fence (2) is set across the arena to lead naturally into the combination (3a and b) which has only to be jumped one way, obviating any special problems with the parallel.

If your arena is narrow you may have to dispense with (2) and (4); instead build (4) in position (*X*) and put the cavalletto (2) at (*Y*). If you then start over (*Y*), coming down the arena, you have three alternatives. On the right rein you have a single fence (5), and on the left rein you have a combination (jumped the opposite way to the one shown) or the fence or cavalletto (1). Any of these alternatives can feed into a different course, each one with different problems — but do watch the parallels and do not jump them from the dangerous side.

Five Fences in a Long, Narrow Arena (1)

It is very useful to build your jumps away from the sides of a long, narrow arena because, in by-passing fences, you can include reasonable turns into the course.

Suggested courses (see Fig. 45)

(1) Starting towards home — (1) and (2) need to be jumped both ways and so have to be upright or low true parallels similar to the example on page 94. Sequence: (1) — (2) — (3a)(3b) — (4) — (2) — (1) — Finish.

(2) Start over (1) again, but increase the difficulty by riding the combination immediately after. By-pass (4), jump (2) and practise the turn between (3b) and (3a) to (4). Or turn across the arena and take fence (1). When riding this course make sure that the horse is on the correct leading leg when landing over (2). The lead is maintained for (4), but a simple change of leg is needed between (2) and (1).

(3) Fence (4) can represent the most formidable obstacle

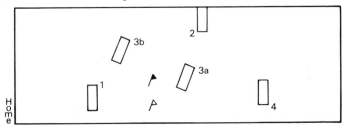

Fig. 45 *Setting five fences in a long narrow arena.*

on the course and, providing it is only jumped the correct way, can be a spread or a sloping fence. The approach to (4) from the opposite end to home is rather cramped, so it would be better to ride the fence from the home end by-passing (1) in so doing. With more practice and a more balanced horse reverse (4) and ride (1)–(2)–(4) after which by-pass (1) and take the combination. Consider if you have the right distance between (4) and (3a) to make it feasible to ride the combination the other way immediately after taking (4), so creating some tricky problems.

Five Fences in a Long, Narrow Arena (2)
In this case all the fences will be jumped only from one direction and so any could be a spread fence (Fig. 46).

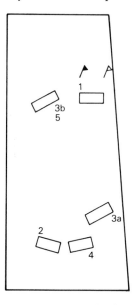

Fig. 46 *Another way of setting out five fences in a narrow arena.*

Starting towards home (1) is the usual small ascending parallel or upright with a set-forward groundline – a low, inviting fence. If you have the material make fence (2) a sloping spread fence (fence (3b) should be a spread as well, if possible).

Coming off the corner and without much of an approach, fence (3a) should be an upright. Fence (3b) could be a true parallel and the distance between the elements here is two strides.

Fence (4) is a difficult upright, perhaps planks or a stile, and is likely to produce inaccuracy on the part of horse and rider after the long canter from (3b). The spirited horse could well be out of control after this long haul.

After (4) take (2) again and line up for (3b) – now used by itself as (5).

If practising a jump-off finish after fence (5) remember not to rush through the flags or you may be unable to stop the horse jumping (1) again.

22 PLANNING YOUR OWN COURSES

However much material you have you will want to use it to the best advantage. That means setting yourself the kind of problems that coursebuilders try to include in their courses in order to cut down the field to a manageable number for the jump-off. Thus you need to develop the mind of a coursebuilder and, while you may not be able to set up a full round of fences, you could plan longer, more demanding, courses and set out parts of them.

To see how a full course is constructed let us look at a typical lay-out for a big competition where many of the fences are near the maximum height. The principles involved are no different from the ones you will encounter with more modest heights at local shows and arenas. (Fig. 47.)

The course consists of three sections:
(1) the entrance section — low, easy, no tricks; followed by
(2) the middle section — bigger fences, problems set with odd turns, alternations of shapes of fence and combinations; and
(3) the finishing section — where fences get big, broad and with chains of related distances and combination distances where those who have survived so far can well be careless and drop a pole or two.

Taking the course, fence by fence, we find:
(1) a simple ascending parallel set low for the class;
(2) a triple bar with a sharp 90° turn beyond it into
(3) a relatively simple two-stride combination.

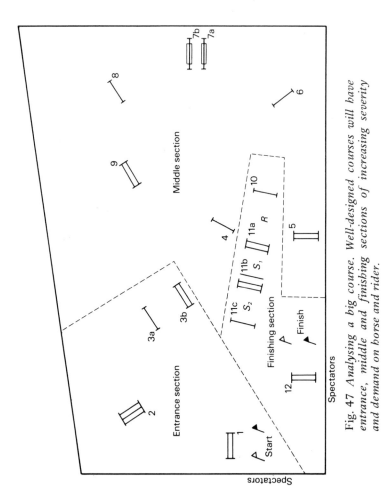

Fig. 47 *Analysing a big course. Well-designed courses will have entrance, middle and finishing sections of increasing severity and demand on horse and rider.*

The triple bar invites the tearaway horse to fly on into the 'open country' beyond, but the combination must be approached straight so the controlled, balanced horse-and-rider combination will be rewarded here. Putting the oxer (3b) to follow the upright (3a) is not, however, a usual practice for novices or ponies.

We now move on to the main body of the course. The upright (4) consists of planks and does not lie on the natural approach line from the combination. The big parallel (5) needs a very straight approach, but this cannot be achieved naturally from landing over (4). Thus a sharp balanced turn on the right rein has to be made if (5) is to be approached with any certainty, then it can be cleared cleanly. After (5) there is a 'gymkhana' turn, again on the right rein, to approach (6), an upright of poles and planks. The reversal of direction is important in this course as the spectators are sited down on the lower left sides and the start and finish action is designed to be there.

A pair of ditches with uprights over them (7a and b) with a one-stride distance between will not be found on many local courses, but a one-stride combination, say, of walls and rails, could replace it. Fence (8) is simple to approach and is something of a bonus, but the parallel (9) is difficult. It is wide and 'upstream' of (8), therefore it will be a calculated risk as to how far to ride beyond (9) before turning to approach it. Fence (9) is the last in the middle section and the big bogey of the course now looms.

At this stage in the course a strong, unruly horse will be keyed up and the long distance from (9) to (10) can make him even more headstrong, especially when time is tight and time-faults loom. To avoid this, build into your practice course at home a sequence of several fences together followed by a long run before the next fence. Come off a turn into this last fence, as that makes the whole thing more difficult. Such ploys, coming late in the course when the field is either over-excited or tending to tire, can be deadly for the chances of many.

The line (10) and (11) is a related distance R followed by a one-stride distance S_1 and a two-stride distance S_2 — they *can* be placed more problematically but not much. Fence (10) is a massive upright which will require considerable effort from the horse before he even tackles the treble. This latter consists of a true parallel (11a) followed by a big triple bar (11b), and finally an upright (11c). The different shapes of fences plus the unequal striding between the elements of this line will eliminate all but the most balanced and athletic of horse—rider combinations. Yet today the top horses do this kind of combination line as a matter of routine. Little wonder that the upper echelons of show-jumping are so sparsely populated compared to the number of young hopefuls who start up the ladder.

When practising at home, you can make lines with related and combination distances in them for the developing horse, but the heights must be kept low or you may well end up over-stretching him and yourself before you are ready for such advanced work.

The horses that have survived the (10)–(11) line have one last obstacle — a big oxer (12). The remarks made about the approach to (9) from (8) apply here, only more so as the horse is tiring — it has had to give almost its all over the line (10) and (11) — and a very carefully judged approach has to be made to (12) to give the animal all the help it needs in order to clear this last obstacle.

These observations should help you to look at the courses you walk with more confidence. In any case they point out the kinds of pitfalls that good course-builders will lay for you. Maybe your courses are on a lesser scale, but they will be of equal severity taking into account the difference that exists between your horse and a top show-jumping horse.

Dissecting the Course

You cannot hope to build anything like the course in Fig. 47 – it merely shows the kinds of problems you should be setting yourself. So, let us take parts of this course and set them in your home arena. Fig. 48a is the entrance section and to build this you will need:

- 7 pairs of wings
- 2 stands
- 1 cavalletto
- 10 poles, or 8 poles and two planks, or 7 poles plus a gate
- 2 sets of hurdles or other fillers

Fence (1) economises on poles by using a solid filler topped by a pole with a set-forward cavalletto in front of it. With an extra pole you could set a concrete-block cavalletto here.

Fence (2) is a triple bar – two pairs of wings plus stands or again a concrete-block leading element. Three poles are required for this.

Fence (3a) is a true parallel with a single pole on both pairs of wings and a groundline pole laid in the leading plane of the fence. The openness of this fence should be overcome with a suitable filler.

Fence (3b) can be any form of upright depending on what you have available. It ought to be a potential bogey made from planks or a gate, but if you have none of these an upright of poles will suffice. Note that the order of the spread and upright is reversed to make it potentially easier to jump for the pony or young horse.

The problems in jumping the above course will include containing the activity of the horse after it has successfully negotiated the triple bar, plus making sure that the correct leading leg is maintained after jumping (2) as there is little room for bringing the horse back to trot to initiate a simple change of leg. The horse can be induced to land with the correct lead by moving your outside leg back behind the girth when in the free-flight phase of the jump, i.e. by using the leg opposite to the leading leg you require.

As this exercise is all on the same bend, the horse should naturally maintain the correct lead, but he may not necessarily do so.

Fig. 48(b) is the first half of the middle section of Fig. 47 where fence (2) has been simulated in position by a cavalletto. This is a tough assignment as you have a sharp turn on the right rein through 120° and then have to meet a combination. Note that in rebuilding the course the order of upright and spread has been reversed. Do not build (3a) and (3b) too high but make them well within your capabilities, because there are more problems to follow.

By altering the arrangement somewhat you can have an alternative fence (4). The one on the right of the direction of jumping is more likely to be ridden in balance than the alternative on the left as there is a change of direction on landing over (3b). In the latter case unless your horse is good at changing legs you will be forced to come back to a few paces of trot before jumping Alt(4) because you need firstly left lead and then right lead.

Fence (4) can be an upright made out of the remnants of Fence (1), and (5) is an ascending parallel made from the triple bar (2) with the third pole laid as a groundline. Fence (6) is a new entry and so requires more material, but if you have constructed a stile it would be very suitable for this fence. However, it still demands an extra pair of wings.

The approach to (5) over (4) will entail some very

Fig. 48 *Home courses based on sections of the full course shown in Fig. 47.*

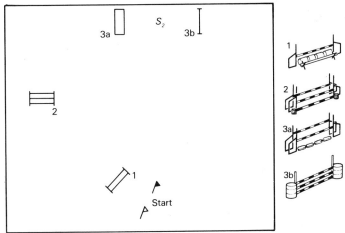

(a) *Re-making the entrance section for home use.*

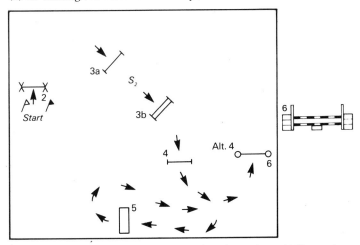

(b) *The lead from the entrance section into the middle section includes some nasty 'gymkhana' turns. The thumb-nail sketches suggest fences that could be built.*

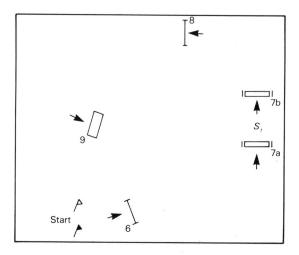

(c) *The middle section of the course re-made for the home arena.*

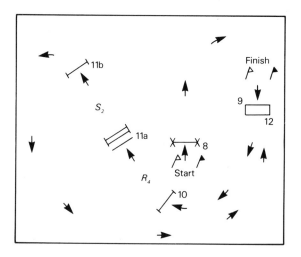

(d) *The finishing section reduced to two fences plus a related and combination chain.*

controlled riding if it is done properly and absolutely demands coming back to trot in order to make the sharp left turn and the, even sharper, right turn required to line up with the parallel (5). You should make (5) something of a test for you and the horse, as if it is too low it will be tempting just to jump it on the angle straight after (4) which is not the object of the exercise.

There is more 'gymkhana' riding to come in order to get back to (6) and all in all this could prove a fairly difficult exercise.

Fig. 48(c) is the second part of the middle section of the course shown in Fig. 47. Here we have a series of turns of different radius on the same rein. The upright (6) is moved so that a clear line leads into the one-stride combination (7). This in turn leads into an upright (8) which can be made easier by moving it more to the left. Eventually it should be jumped in the position shown. It should be large-ish so that you really have to keep control, land on the correct lead and maintain impulsion round the corner. Then we have a parallel (9) which, being well upstream of (8), has to be carefully approached. It is better at first to ride too far on and to keep (9) low. Then practise making the turn as you might wish to in a jump-off, remembering that if you cut the corner too sharply you may not manage the spread. The horse may well refuse to take off at such an angle and if he does so then who can blame him.

Fig. 48(d) is the finishing section, which obviously has to be simplified because there is unlikely to be enough material to build a related distance and a treble even if there is enough room. Anyway, that is a tougher assignment than the beginner can be expected to tackle. In order to approach the line of fences re-make fence (8) as a starting fence and put (9) in the same relative position as before, but such that it leads fairly neatly into the upright (10) which is followed at, say, a four-stride related distance by a triple bar and then a two-stride combination distance S to another upright. That upright can be built up after initial practice in maintaining rhythm and impulsion over the line at moderate heights. You could then retake (9) the opposite way to finish as shown.

This finishing section is a real test of your ability to ride controlled turns on both reins. Also, the long run from (11) to (12) will have the unruly horse galloping on and arriving unbalanced and careless at the last fence. Such long distances need to be ridden with great care as they can spoil an otherwise good round simply by allowing the euphoria of the 'chase' to get to you and the horse.

You will be able to find in books plans of courses set for top classes and you can just as easily dissect these plans and build them in sections knowing that you are thereby including in your own courses the kinds of problems found in varying degrees in any coursebuilder's repertoire. Otherwise, you could spend time sketching or memorising parts of the courses you see at shows and use them as a basis for your own home coursebuilding.

PART FOUR

MAKING YOUR OWN JUMPS

23 MATERIALS AND EQUIPMENT

It is not difficult to make wings, stands, stiles, hurdles etc. In the following pages are instructions for producing various items of equipment, selected for their cheapness, effectiveness and their ease of construction. Perhaps the most difficult job is accurately drilling the uprights; a drill-stand is a great asset for this purpose.

An essential tool is an electric drill with a two-speed facility and an assortment of wood and metal bits. It saves time and effort if you have an electric handsaw as well, but you can still do most jobs with an ordinary carpenter's saw. Apart from that you could very well be glad of a portable workbench which has jaws that will grip most thicknesses of wood you may be using. Apart from these 'capital' items your basic toolkit should consist of hammer and nails, spanner for tightening bolts, a hacksaw, a screwdriver and screws.

Wood

Apart from odd lengths you might find at home or which you might have bought as a job-lot from a market, the timber you should purchase for home jump construction should be softwood. Softwood is now available in metric equivalents of the more familiar feet-and-inch sizes. At least this is so for width and thickness, but not for length where the shortest length produced is 1.8 metres (5ft 10⅞ ins). Longer lengths go up in steps of 30cm, i.e. the nearest equivalent to a foot.

The smallest size of softwood normally sold is the equivalent of 3ins wide by ½in. thick and this is a 'sawn' size. Sawn wood is rough and cheaper than planed and if finish does not matter, buy sawn. However, planed sizes will be 3mm less both ways than the sizes you quote. Thus a planed upright asked for as 4ins x 2ins will actually be something less than an eighth of an inch smaller all round.

There are very few jobs in home fencebuilding where size is critical, so you can ask for wood in feet and inches bearing in mind the following points. All metric widths are slightly less than their British standard values ('slightly' means a matter of 1/10in. or less). Thicknesses are slightly more up to 1¼ins thick after which they are slightly less.

So, for example, the wood size of 3ins x ½in. recommended for making bale-cups on page 155, will in fact be sawn to 7.5cm x 1.6cm which is 2.95ins x 0.6in. Such variations are of no consequence, but it always helps to take a rule with you when you buy timber especially for the lengths. As metric lengths are so different, here is a conversion table for them:

Sawn length	1.8m	2.1m	2.4m	2.7m	3.0m
Imperial equivalent	5ft 10½ins	6ft 10½ins	7ft 10½ins	8ft 10ins	9ft 10ins
Sawn length	3.3m	3.6m	4.2m	4.5m	
Imperial equivalent	10ft 9½ins	11ft 9½ins	13ft 9ins	14ft 9ins	

(In the above table Imperial equivalents have been rounded down to the nearest half an inch, therefore you may get slightly more than the length quoted, but you should not get less.)

Plywoods and Boards

For many filling jobs, or if you decide to make a wall etc., you will probably plump for plywood. For durability buy external-quality ply; the greater the number of layers in the ply the stronger it will be. Horses, especially in training, have a great propensity for stubbing their feet against the bottom of walls and other fillers, so this part of the fence needs to be strong. However, cost is always important and the thicker forms of multi-ply can be quite expensive especially when of external quality.

For economy you might consider chipboard, which would cover a large area at a modest cost. However this is not at all a good idea as chipboard shatters so easily when struck. Blockboard is somewhat better but is heavy compared to ply and again will damage fairly easily in use. All in all plywood will serve you best for fillers.

It is a matter of cost and convenience what plywood you choose, but ply that is a quarter of an inch thick is not really suitable. If you happen upon some thin ply, such as old tea-chests, and it is all you can afford to use, make do by supporting it well behind with battens to strengthen it.

Adhesives

Rather than nail bale-cups, hurdles etc. together, you could glue them, but you need a proper wood glue that will stand up to the stresses and the outdoor life. The best is probably a urea-based glue such as Aerolite or Cascomite, both of which are very strong and will allow you to slide and re-position the wood which contact adhesives do not allow. These urea glues are also capable of filling the inevitable gaps between pieces of sawn wood.

You may be offered a casien glue such as Casco, but this does not have the gap-filling attributes of Cascomite. Perhaps the toughest bond of all is made by epoxy-resin glues such as Araldite and Bostik 7, but these are not as simple to use as the urea-based adhesives.

When positioning and leaving surfaces to bond, it helps to drive in a nail or two to keep the surfaces in place. If you do not drive the nails fully home they can be pulled out again when the bonding is complete. They *can* of course be driven home, but they will add nothing to the strength of the well-made bonds of modern adhesives.

A really useful item is one of the electronic glue guns that are now on the market. In these, solid cylinders of adhesive are thrust through an electronically heated section and the liquid glue emerges in a simple, clean and efficient manner just where you want it.

Paints and Painting

However battered such things as barrels and cans may be it is remarkable what a coat of paint will do. When you make wooden accessories for your course you will in most cases want to paint them. If the paint is to stay on, you will have to buy oil-based paint and put it on in warm, dry weather. An undercoat of plain white, water-based emulsion (which is about the cheapest paint you can buy) works quite adequately although the paint will not stay on as permanently as it will if the wood is primed first, then given an oil-based undercoat, followed by a gloss top-coat.

If all that sounds like a lot of hard work remember that poles, etc. take a massive amount of punishment and if you take the trouble to paint them properly to start with, you won't have to do them again for a long time.

Rustic items can be given a coat of creosote, but it

takes a long time to dry out – if it ever does – and horses have been known to while away the hours chewing at creosoted poles and hurdles etc. It is best, I find, to leave rustic things just as they are. You can even leave the bark on until it flakes, then remove it all if you can.

Some recommend that when you have cleaned the outside of a steel barrel a special metal primer should be applied, but I have never had any problems of flaking paint by just using two coats of gloss. Again the painting needs to be carried out when the weather is dry and warm if lasting results are to be achieved. Mid-winter is not the time to be painting unless you can get in under cover and the weather is mild and relatively dry – a combination you rarely get in the winter.

Drills and Bits

An electric power drill is to be found in most house-holds today and you will not be able to make many of the items described here without one. As already mentioned, a drill-stand, while not essential, is a great asset if you wish to put holes accurately in uprights etc.

Bits are of two main kinds. Firstly, metal bits will double as wood bits providing you withdraw the bit every so often to clear the 'swarf'. Metal bits are relatively short and so will often not fully penetrate deeper thicknesses of wood. This can be overcome by drilling from both sides, but great care is needed in positioning. Further, most metal bits for domestic use will not go to sizes over about $\frac{3}{8}$ in. The chuck on most drills will not take larger sizes and ½in. is about the largest that can be accommodated by domestic drills.

Secondly, you will need some wood bits designed to be used with domestic drills. These need to be run at the slower of the two speeds which most drills give you these days. They are long enough to do most wood-boring jobs and can be bought in diameters of over an inch if you want them. In building fences about the largest size required will be $5/8$ in. Other sizes will be dictated by the size of bolts you intend to use.

If you can only use a hand-brace then the bits designed for use with power drills are no good and you will need the helical or other form of low-speed wood bit.

24 BALE CUPS

Simple bale cups are so easy to make that anyone who has a saw, a hammer and a few nails can put them together in a matter of minutes.

You use 3in. wide by ½in. thick 'sawn' timber and each cup needs two lengths that are about 2ft long, and two cross members that are 8½ins long. Cut these and nail them together as shown in Fig. 49. The only critical measurement is the 2½ins between the lengths as an ordinary pole fits snugly into this width, but in such a way that it can be knocked out.

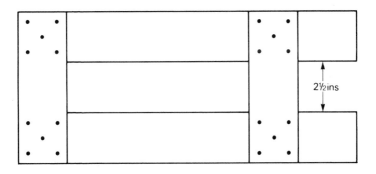

Fig. 49 *Plan of a simple bale cup.*

As these cups do not allow you much variation in height you can also make 'blocked' cups. These require blocks which are 9ins by 8ins by about 2ins thick. Cut a notch in each block as shown in Fig. 50 and a standard pole will rest in the notch giving a pole height about 6ins higher than with a plain bale cup. Nail the blocks onto simple cups as is evident from Photo 1 (page 24).

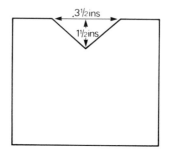

Fig. 50 *Cross-section of blocked bale cup.*

25 STILES

It is very easy to produce special cups that will take square-section rails and so make a stile that will fit onto any of your wings (Fig. 51). Buy three planed bars

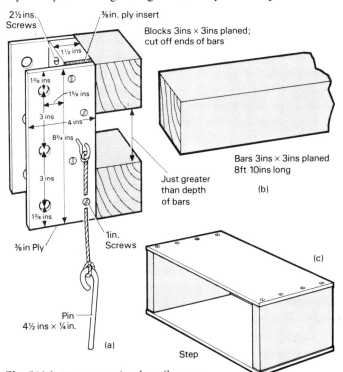

Fig. 51(a) *How to make the stile cups.*
(b) *The bars are easy to make but remember to chamfer their edges.*
(c) *A step is simple to make but is not essential.*

3m long and of square section 3ins x 3ins. Cut four 3in. lengths off each bar which will leave a bar about 8ft 10ins long. For each pair of cups you need enough $^3/_8$ in. thick plywood to make four side pieces 4ins x 8¾ins plus two inserts. You need two 8¾in. main supports, which are the same width as that of your wings. That width plus the insert will ensure the cups slide easily on the wing uprights. It is best here to screw (or glue) the pieces together as shown. The pins are roofing hooks cut to a length of about 4½ins and the holes for them need be only $^3/_8$ in. but they must be centred 1$^5/_8$ ins in from the inner face of the support.

Chamfer the sharp edges of the stile bars with a plane or Surform so that the horse does not cut his feet on them. It is not essential to have a step — it is merely an added refinement.

26 PLANKS

Riders hate planks — their horses always seem to be knocking them down. It is therefore essential that you train your horse to pay the same respect to planks as he does to poles.

For the home builder without metalworking facilities the biggest construction problem when making planks is the metal supporting brackets that fit on each end. I will describe how to make these as they are a standard kind of fitment, but there is an effective and much easier way of providing supports which fit standard flat cups and have the added advantage of resisting the tendency of allowing the planks to swing in the wind.

It might seem that driving a heavy nail into each end of a plank will make an adequate support with little trouble and expense. Let me warn at the outset that you will be very disappointed in the result: the plank will never stay vertical and will swing alarmingly in the wind. It is essential that the end supports have a broad base on which to rest so you will need to buy two pairs of gate latches from an ironmonger's or DIY store, plus four 1½ ins. x ¼in. coach bolts (Photo 7). If they are coach bolts they will be threaded all the way down and if 1½in. bolts are not available you can always buy longer ones and cut off the surplus. You may need to open up the holes in the latches to take the bolts.

It is pointless buying the plank timber less than an inch in thickness. Even this may tend to warp with time and will not sit happily on the cups. By mixing planks with poles in your fence you can produce the desired

Photo 7 *Using gate latches (see top plank) to support light planks. If you use heavier planks you must make brackets as shown in Fig. 52.*

effect with just a couple of planks, the widest of which could well be as little as 6ins wide. The actual length will be 2ins less each end than the overall required length — see Fig. 2(a). Thus 9ft planks will be 8ft 8ins long which is very close to the 2.7m length that is one of the preferred metric lengths and you will only need to cut off a matter of 2¼ins to obtain the correct length. It follows that a 10ft plank will need to be 9ft 8ins long (close to a 3m length) and a 12ft one, 11ft 8ins long (close to a 3.6m length).

To get an absolutely correct height the top of the plank needs to be 5ins above the line of the hole in the cup and so it needs to be 3½ins above the bottom of the latches. However, these dimensions are correct only for 7in. planks. Draw a horizontal line 3½ins below the top of the plank at both ends and on both sides and use these to line up the latches as you drill the holes. It is worth putting just one hole through and bolting up lightly so as to ensure the latches are horizontal when you drill the second hole. You will find that on a 1in. thick plank this form of support will fit neatly onto standard flat cups. It is also very simple to do and that makes up for it not being as mechanically strong as the more conventional bracket. For other depths of plank use the depth (*b*) given below as a guide to where to place the latches.

If you have no welding facilities your farrier can probably help you have brackets made up as shown in Fig. 52. With the depth of plank *A* = 6ins, the dimensions (*a*), (*b*) and (*c*) are 6ins, 4½ins and 3½ins respectively. If *A* = 4½ins then the dimensions are 5ins, 3½ins and 2½ins while for a 7in. wide plank they are 6ins, 5½ins and 3½ins. They need to be drilled through and bolted, as shown, with a couple of substantial screws as well to help hold the upright parts of the brackets. Three sizes

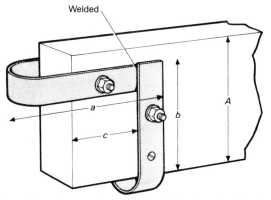

Fig. 52 *Making the standard form of bracket for heavy planks made from scaffold boards or similar. The main support should be the same width as the uprights.*

Photo 8(a) and (b) *Ideas for designs you can paint on your home planks.*

are quoted above because if you want to really go to town on your plank jump then a graded set of widths as above will look very good.

What you paint on the planks is up to you. It can be simple bands of alternating colour and white; shark's teeth; or an arresting design of your own like the playing-card planks in the photographs. However you paint them make sure that the elements match and put something different on each side.

27 BARREL WINGS AND UPRIGHTS

Oil barrels or similar are not difficult to come by and even if you can only get damaged ones a coat of paint will make them look good again. Let us assume you have managed to acquire a couple of barrels, have cleaned them up and painted them. As they naturally fall into three bands then paint them that way too, i.e. top and bottom one colour, say red, with a light contrasting colour in the middle. With the bulges to guide you it is not difficult to get the lines between the colours straight, but as with all contrast painting make sure that one colour is dry before you paint over it with another.

Each upright consists of 4ins x 2ins planed wood about 5ft or more high, which can be drilled with holes every 3ins, the first being 13ins off the ground. Such uprights will give heights of 1ft 6ins upwards in steps of 3ins and will be compatible with the uprights on wings sold by saddlery companies. However some builders of jumping equipment may be drilling their uprights at 10cm intervals which means that every time you go up or down a hole you are changing the height by just under 4ins. My own view is that, as with so many other things that are human orientated (as opposed to science orientated), the Imperial units are best and certainly feet and inches are far more compatible with ease of use in the horse world than the metre which starts off at over a yard and has no smaller integral number units such as the three feet of the yard.

If you prefer or need to drill uprights with metric

heights then the first hole must be 37.3cm off the ground, which will give a lowest height of pole of 0.5m or 1ft 7½ins. After that each hole is 10cm above the one below it.

It is essential to set the holes the correct distance in from the face of the upright or the cups will sag or, worse, not fit at all. If you do not use some sort of guide it is very easy to drill them at irregular distances in; the following idea not only provides such a guide, but makes some serviceable cups at the same time.

As lengths of timber are now in metres, when you buy suitable lengths for a pair of uprights you will get two 2.1m lengths which are just over 6ft 10ins. Since you will not want them that high you will have to cut 16ins off the end. Saw from the 16in. length two 7in. lengths, which will leave you with a piece about 2ins wide. The thickness of 4ins x 2ins planed uprights is less than 2ins as it was 2ins before the planing machine got to work on it. So if you nail the 2in. wide odd piece between the 7in. side pieces as shown in Fig. 53 you will have the makings of a cup. Taking great care to keep the drill vertical (and here you really need the drill-stand mentioned earlier — see Photo 9) drill a ⅜in. hole 1⅝ins in from the spacer. This will then fit standard uprights if required. For pins buy roofing hooks as shown in Fig. 51. Cut them so that about an inch or so projects and close up the hook end into a loop either by compressing in a vice or by hammering the hook shut. Drive a staple into a suitable place on the side of the wooden cup and attach the pin with string (bale twine is quite suitable). See Photo 13.

You will find that a 3in. or 4in. pole rests well on these cups and as you were forced to buy a greater length of 4ins x 2ins than you needed they are cheap to make. If you already have wings with uprights then measure the thickness of the thickest you have, and ensure that the spacing piece is wide enough so enabling you to use your wooden cups on all of your wings. It is very frustrating to have things on your course that only fit certain other things. It all adds to the work involved and makes you less inclined to do the job properly. So aim for interchangeability and no double standards.

You can now use one of your wooden cups as a template for marking the positions of holes in any other

Photo 9 *Using a drill-stand to make the holes in the uprights.*

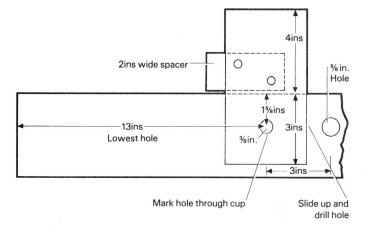

Fig. 53 *A design for a wooden block cup that also serves as a template for marking the position of the holes in uprights.*

uprights you wish to make. The $^3/_8$ in. hole is just right to take a pencil. Mark all the positions — it helps to have given the upright a coat of undercoat first — and then use a $^5/_8$ ins. wood bit to make the holes. Drill through onto a metal plate so that the bit does not come straight through and so tear the edges of the hole. The point of the bit will have marked each hole on the underside and then you can turn the upright over and drill again, so producing sharp edges to your holes both sides.

A really cheap, but serviceable form of upright that is very suitable for schooling is illustrated in Fig. 54. The uprights are of 'sawn' wood 4ft 6ins high and 3ins wide by 2ins thick. They are fitted to a barrel using roofing hooks as shown. With a hacksaw cut a notch out of the rims of the barrel top and bottom to just accommodate the thickness of the hook — this is essential to the final rigidity of the set-up (Photo 10.)

Taking care to see that the distance between the

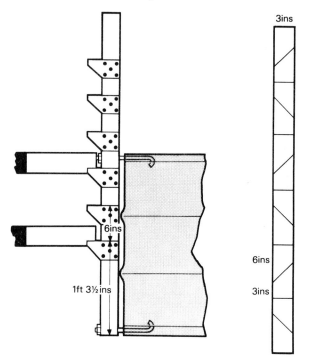

Fig. 54(a) *A form of upright that does not need drilling.*
(b) *How to cut out six pairs of blanks for the supports. Use a length of ½in. thick by 3ins wide plywood that is 4ft 6ins long.*

hooks will be exactly the same as the depth of the drum, drill two ³⁄₈ in. holes and fit the roofing hooks having opened up the hooks somewhat. If you do not do this you will not be able to slot them into the ³⁄₈ in. holes drilled in the top and bottom of the barrel. Before you drill these holes fit the whole thing together so that you get the holes in the right place. Centre-punch the positions to stop the drill wandering when you first start to drill. Then you can knock the hooks into the

Photo 10 *Fitting uprights to the barrels with roofing hooks.*

holes and tighten up. Pull them in tight — you need washers under the nuts — and then cut off the surplus with a hacksaw.

Now get a length of ½in. thick plywood. It needs to be 3ins wide and a total of 4ft 6ins long. Mark it out as shown in Fig. 54(b) and cut out the six pairs of supports. Mark the top of the first one at 1ft 3½ins from the ground and nail it on. This will give you a pole height of 1ft 6ins, but the inevitable consequences of the design mean that you cannot set the next support closer than 6ins; however you have to weigh such a slight disadvantage against the ease of construction. Make sure you cut the nail points off as shown or they could be dangerous. See Photo 11.

This is about the cheapest and easiest form of wing you could hope to make, but they are, I feel, only stop-gaps until you can get some standard wings. Standard uprights are drilled at 3in. centres to take normal cups.

Photo 11 *A simple upright — perhaps a stop-gap before acquiring standard wings.*

They can be fitted with roofing hooks to barrels just as easily as the cheap form. Barrel wings make useful additions to any course wherever it is being built. They take an awful lot of punishment and do not easily blow over in the wind.

The idea of using roofing hooks is perfectly serviceable, but bolting uprights directly to the barrels is another way of doing it. This involves removing the top of the barrel. In most cases the top is made of thinner material than the bottom and is therefore easier to cut.

Cutting out the end of a barrel is not an easy task,

but if you can do it it helps lighten the wings and ensures that your uprights are absolutely rigidly fixed to the barrels. You need a 'cold chisel' and a heavy hammer plus some stout gloves for all the times you might miss the chisel. You then have to warn all and sundry about the noise you are about to make and slowly cut out the top rather in the manner of an old-fashioned tin-opener. Make sure that whatever was in the barrel is not going to contaminate you or the environment, especially where there are horses or other livestock. Wash out the interior over a drain so that no toxic matter is allowed to soak into the ground.

Photo 12 *Using barrels as fillers. They must be made safe with the ground pole to stop them rolling.*

28 WINGS FROM TYRES

Old tyres are always available. If there are none to be had from your own resources or from friends, then tyre companies usually have piles of old tyres that they are happy to see the back of. Thus tyres for the base of wings is a cheap and attractive proposition.

After several development designs the one I am going to describe is serviceable and simple to make. Do not get tyres that are too small or too big, and make sure that their walls are still sound.

You need a length of 4ins x 2ins which does not need to be planed (but looks a lot better if it is); drill this for cups as described on page 167. Measure the distance A (see Fig. 55) in the matching pair of tyres you have selected for the bases and cut two pieces of 3ins x 3ins which are 2ins shorter than A. This will enable you to get the assembly in and out of the tyre as you make it up.

Using a 5/16in. wood bit, drill through the 3in. bars and the 4ins x 2ins upright as shown, leaving 4ins of the former ahead of the face of the upright and enough of the latter sticking out below the bars to contact the lower rim of the tyre when the assembly is bolted up. Leave rather more than might appear necessary to allow for the fact that the whole thing will rise somewhat when assembled. Pull the bars and the upright together using an 8in. long roofing hook.

Cut a piece of 6ins x 1in. which is 8ins long (C), and another about 18ins long (B). The latter needs to be measured from the tyres you have so that it just about

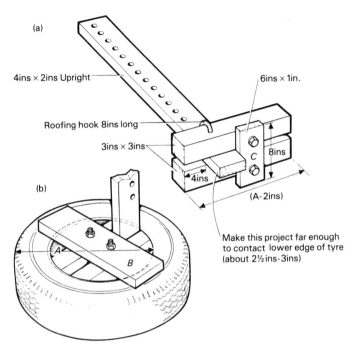

(a)

4ins × 2ins Upright

6ins × 1in.

Roofing hook 8ins long

3ins × 3ins

8ins

C

(b)

4ins

(A-2ins)

A

B

Make this project far enough to contact lower edge of tyre (about 2½ins-3ins)

Fig. 55(a) *How to assemble the portion that will be inserted in the tyre.*
(b) *Make the bars 2ins less than the length A and cut a piece of 6in. x 1in. wood (B) which via the bolts shown in C will pull the assembly tightly together.*

contacts the circular moulding on the outer edge of the wall of the tyre. Making quite sure that both these pieces snugly contact the upright, drill through *B*, *C* and the bars with your 5/16in. bit to take two 6in. x ¼in. bolts. Having painted the pieces assemble all the parts except for *B* and insert them in the tyre. As you stand the assembly up put another piece of wood under *C* to keep the bolts pushed home when you put on *B*. Make sure that you have washers on both ends of the bolts as the strength of the assembly lies in how tightly these bolts are pulled up and you do not want to pull the bolt heads into the wood.

As you tighten up make sure that the face of the upright contacts the rims of the tyres top and bottom. Then the upright will be caught between the rims and the pieces of wood *B* and *C* so preventing it wobbling. The finished wing is shown in Photo 13 and while you do not *have* to paint the walls of the tyres white it certainly helps the appearance.

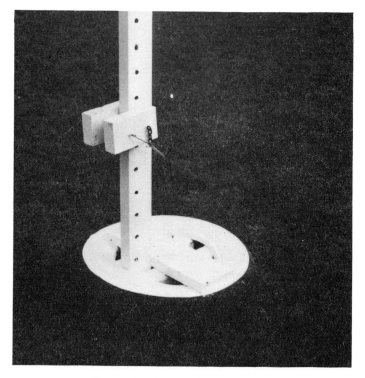

Photo 13 *The completed tyre wing.*

Photo 14 *Dangerous. Never use tyres stacked this way as a filler. If the horse puts a leg into or onto the pile of tyres they could collapse sideways and he could break his limb.*

29 HURDLES

Simple Hurdles

It is amongst the easiest of construction jobs to make a set of three 2ft high hurdles to fill a 9ft space or four to fill a 12ft space. Each one needs to be just less than 3ft wide overall, which includes the feet. If you have, however, standardised on 10ft poles then each hurdle needs to be just under 3ft 4ins in overall width to fill that space. (Fig. 56.)

We will describe the ones to fill 9ft which will be about 2ft 11¾ins wide. You will require three lengths of 1.8m (5ft 11ins) and three lengths of 2.1m (7ft 10½ins) of 6in. x 1in. timber. You cannot make do with lighter timber than this unless you radically alter the design; do not forget that the hurdles have to cope with all the wear and tear of a jumping paddock.

From the 1.8m lengths you can cut six cross-pieces 2ft 10ins wide with little wastage. From each 2.1m length you can cut two 2ft uprights and then have a piece over which, if divided in two, will make the two feet which will be about 1ft 5¼ins wide. This width is not critical.

Nail (or glue) them together as shown making sure that the ends of the cross-pieces come flush with the uprights so that you have a flat surface of large area on which to nail the feet. Nail the feet securely to the ends of the hurdles and again, if possible, glue them as well. If you use fairly hefty wire nails drill small holes for them first to prevent the wood splitting.

Obviously if you have 12ft to fill you will need an

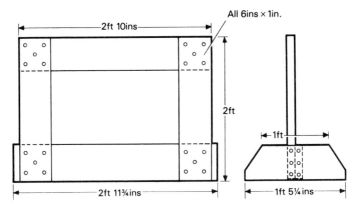

Fig. 56(a) *How to make simple hurdles out of 6in. x 1in. wood.*
(b) *How to shape the feet and fix them (viewed from the outside).*

extra piece of each length.

The hurdles are open which means that they are less likely to be blown over by the wind, but if you wish you can fill them in with plywood.

Low Hurdles

Here is another simple way of making small hurdles, using planks that are 4ins deep by ¾ins thick by 3ft long. See Fig. 57.

For each 3ft hurdle cut four pieces of 1in. x 1in. battening which are 13ins long and nail the assembly together as shown in the diagrams.

The feet are cut from 1in. thick board that is 20ins wide and 8ins deep. Shape the feet as shown and make two saw cuts in each which are 3ins deep and just wide enough for the lower plank of the hurdle to slot into. Chisel out the slot and slip the hurdle into it. Nail through the feet into the battens and if possible glue the feet on as well.

Make as many hurdles as you need to fill the width

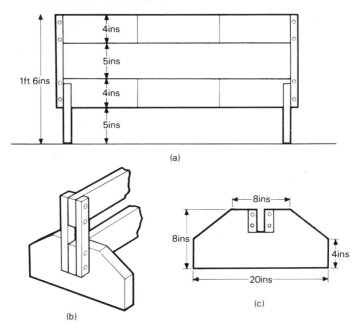

Fig. 57(a) *Side elevation of the complete plank hurdle.*
(b) *How the ends are constructed.*
(c) *Dimensions of the feet.*

of poles and planks you are using, but if you have 10ft long poles then you would be advised to make two hurdles each 5ft long. These hurdles stand 1ft 6ins from the ground and again can be used on their own to form part of schooling grids or small jumps where required.

Rustic Hurdles

I made the hurdles described here from poles that had been bought from the Forestry Commission and had lain in the pile for a year or so. That is the best way, but you may not want to wait that long. If you use the poles as soon as cut you will have to put up with the fact that they might develop 'shakes'. If the bark is sound you can leave it on, but the rougher lumps and remains of branches etc. should be cut off with a saw or a sharp axe and then smoothed with a plane or Surform.

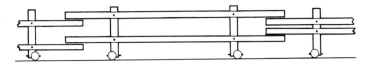

Fig. 58 *Hurdles. The design on the left is in many ways better than that on the right but either will give a lower height and can also slot into the one shown in the middle.*

You are certainly going to need a good saw for this job and a wood bit that is clearance size for some hefty bolts which should not be less than $\frac{3}{8}$ in. diameter. The poles need to be about 14ft or 15ft long and if you get ones that are perhaps 20ft or so the thick ends, that you cut off to form the rails, will make good uprights and feet. However you will not make enough of them that way so you will need to select the thicker of the poles you have to cut up into uprights and feet.

To make each hurdle you need:

2 x 14ft long x 4in. diameter rails

2 x 3ft high by 4in.—5in. diameter uprights

2 x 2ft 6ins long by 5in.—6in. diameter feet

6 x $\frac{3}{8}$ in. bolts whose lengths you will have to determine when you have cut the slots in the rails, uprights and feet.

This may be a rustic job, but there are certain important things that you must take care to get right if the hurdles are to be strong and withstand transportation as well as bangs from horses' hooves. The strength of the hurdles is in the neat fit of the slots you cut in, say, the bottom of the uprights to take the corresponding slots in the feet (Fig. 59). Cut the slot in a foot so that it is just less than the diameter (*d*) of the upright – Fig. 59 (c). Having done this then, and only then, offer it to

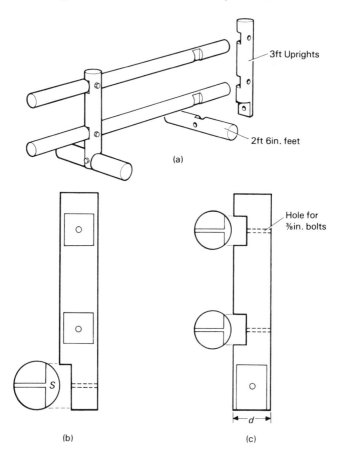

Fig. 59(a) *Putting rustic hurdles together.*
(b) *Slot S, cut in the foot, should match the corresponding slot in the bottom of the upright.*
(c) *The slots in the rails and uprights should also fit snugly together.*

Photo 15 *A pair of the hurdles arranged as a simple ascending parallel.*

the upright and mark where the top of the slot comes on the latter. Allow a little below the bottom of the upright so as to ensure you rest on the foot and not on the upright. When the two slots marry together snugly then drill them through making sure that you get someone to help you hold them together. It is unlikely that you will be able to drill the hole right through in one go. So make sure that you follow the line of the hole you have already made (and which has marked the upright underneath) so that the two surfaces of the slots fit neatly together. If you do not take great care over this you will find the heavy hurdles soon begin to wobble however much you have tightened the bolts.

In the case of the bolts you must gauge the length from the size of wood you are using after you have cut the slots in it. It is important to fit washers of sufficient area to make sure you can pull the bolts up really tight without pulling the heads into the wood.

In cutting the slots you can get a uniform depth by using a power saw that allows you to set the correct depth of cut. These can be hired from firms who specialise in the hire of power and other tools. You will have to chip out the unwanted wood and so you will need a chisel and mallet. Aim to make the finish reasonably flat, but it does not have to be smooth as the roughness will aid friction and so help to prevent movement between the parts when bolted up.

30 TRIPLE-BAR WINGS

Having some stands on which you can build parallels without having to use other wings is a great asset on a home course, and the ones shown here have been proved to be very serviceable and are easy to make, Further, their open-work construction makes them relatively light but less likely to blow over in the wind than a more solid construction.

All the uprights are 4ins x 2ins planed wood and once built the basic box is 4ft high and 2ft square. See Fig. 60(a). The tall upright is 5ft 6ins high, but if you do not anticipate going to heights of over 4ft then both uprights could be 4ft. The method of construction is evident from the diagram and for strength the cross-members (A) at the bottom also need to be 4ins x 2ins and should be bolted to the uprights. All the rest of the cross-members are made in 4ins x 1in. timber.

The 'St Andrew's cross' pieces (B) are put in to make the appearance more solid. They should be 3ins x ¼in. ply and nailed onto the uprights so that they do not interfere with the holes. There is enough width in standard cups to accommodate the extra ¼in. thickness if you decide to carry the ply across the width of the uprights and then drill through to complete the hole you have covered up.

A very important contribution to the strength of the whole assembly is the square of ³⁄₈ in. ply nailed into the base which prevents the assembly twisting when in use.

You can construct small stands of the kind shown for a triple-bar arrangement, but the stands can be used just

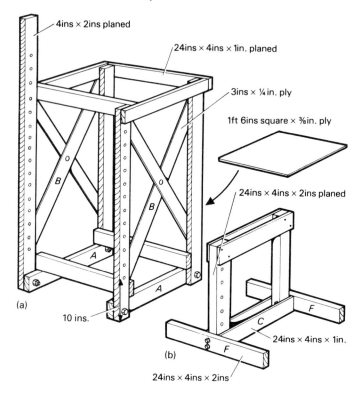

4ins × 2ins planed

24ins × 4ins × 1in. planed

3ins × ¼in. ply

1ft 6ins square × ⅜in. ply

24ins × 4ins × 2ins planed

B

B

A

A

O

O

(a)

10 ins.

24ins × 4ins × 1in.

C

F

F

(b)

24ins × 4ins × 2ins

Fig. 60(a) *Construction of triple-bar wings.*
(b) *The stands that make the ground-line of the triple bar which can be used on their own for other purposes.*

as well for low jumps in schooling grids — Fig. 60(b). It is very easy to knock these up and (as usual) the biggest job is drilling the uprights. However, it is essential that the feet (*F*) are bolted firmly to the uprights and this must be done before the pieces (*C*) of 4ins x 1in. are nailed on. If you wish you can improve the appearance with 'St Andrew's cross' pieces of ply so paralleling the same feature in the main wings.

Even if you cannot contemplate making the big box wings, four of the small stands make a very helpful addition to your store of gymnastic jumping materials.

For each pair of boxes in the metric standard lengths you need:

in 4ins x 2ins	3 lengths of 2.4m which will give six lengths just under 4ft; 2 lengths of 3m from which you can get two 2ft lengths plus a 5ft 10ins upright.
in 4ins x 1in.	4 lengths of 1.8m each of which will cut up into three lengths of just under 2ft (1ft 11½ins)
in ¼in. ply	4 lengths of 2.7m each of which will cut into two 4ft 5ins lengths
bolts	8 of 4ins x ³⁄₈ in.

For each pair of stands you need:

in 4ins x 2ins	2 lengths of 2.4m each of which will cut into two 2ft lengths leaving two 1ft 11ins lengths for the feet
	2 lengths of 2.4m each of which will cut into four lengths of 1ft 11½ins
bolts	8 of 6ins x ¼in.

31 BRUSH BOXES FROM PALLETS

The pallets I found to make the brush boxes shown in Photo 16 were rather damaged at the bottom, but not greatly on the top and as the latter is the important part they were perfectly suitable. They were 48ins by 40ins and so they cut up into two halves that were 4ft wide by 20ins high.

That is a very suitable size for jumping courses because two 4ft widths will all but fill a 9ft fence while three will completely fill a 12ft one. Turn the dimensions round and cut them so that they are 2ft high and 40ins wide and then three will exactly fill a 10ft width.

Although Photo 16 shows the saw-cut being made before the pallet was dismantled it can be done either way. In retrospect it would have been easier to take the bottom slats and blocks off first and then to have cut the top panel in two. However, take care how you dismantle the pallet.

You can minimise the danger of splitting the wood by first driving a wedge into the edges to be separated, as shown in Fig. 61. A light axe driven in with a heavy hammer is very suitable for this job. Having opened a gap, saw through the nails with a hacksaw. This way you will end up with very few split ends to the wood. You need at least one of the bottom slats intact so as to make the feet. The slats I separated from these pallets were 4ins wide and 40ins long so they cut up into 20in. feet very nicely and that length is just right.

You may find that there are nails in the way of cutting

Photo 16 *Cut the top of the pallet in half, having first separated it from the bottom. An almost completed brush box is shown in the background.*

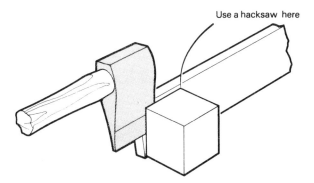

Use a hacksaw here

Fig. 61 *Separating parts of the pallet. First use a light axe to create a gap then saw through the opening with a hacksaw.*

the top panel in half in which case dismantle the pallet before you try to cut the panel. Having cut the nails off with a hacksaw you can then drive them out easily with a punch or another big nail.

It is evident from Photo 16 how and where you use the spacing blocks and once you have done the difficult bit of separating the two sections the rest is easy. I painted alternate slats green and left the others rustic, and they looked quite good. If you cannot obtain any brush the boxes make good solid hurdles used as they are.

Use the left-over slats from the bottom of the pallet to fill in the ends so that the brush does not spill out.

PART FIVE

CROSS-COUNTRY AT HOME

32 USING RUSTIC HURDLES

Cross-country fences must be solid, inviting and safe. They must also be something like the obstacles you will find around the countryside. They will almost without exception be rustic in nature and the more natural they look the better.

There is, however, a very big snag for the rider who cannot have access to someone's cross-country course and that is the usual one of getting practice and introducing the horse to the kinds of fences and problems he will have to negotiate out on courses. The only alternative very often is an impossible one — build your own course. If you pick up a book on building cross-country obstacles it is immediately obvious that such an alternative is quite out of the question. Firstly, you probably haven't the materials, the tools, or the physical strength to build such solid fences. Secondly, where do you build them?

While it will entail some outlay, some work and then some humping about, these problems may be overcome by building moveable rustic hurdles (see page 178). You can go quite a long way with just four such hurdles although six is better and they are not difficult to make. You can then set these up in your own paddock if you cannot get any other facility. However, it may be possible (if you underline the non-permanent nature of the fences you will build) to persuade a local farmer or landowner who has a coppice or similar to let you set up your fences in more natural surroundings for a while. I am certain that non-horsey landowners would be more prepared to co-operate with riders if the latter were careful to introduce no permanent material and were prepared to take the lot away when requested. In any case portable hurdles will provide a possible answer to that often impossible question of where to gain cross-country experience. They could also double as a jumping lane and as dividers between schooling and grazing parts of your paddock.

The first consideration is to decide what height you want the top rail of the hurdles to be. It is wise not to be too ambitious, remember these are practice fences and you should be aiming to develop confidence in yourself and the horse over modest obstacles — height can come later. If you intend to build four hurdles as a start then have the top rail at two heights, one pair say at 2ft 9ins or 3ft and the other 6ins lower, i.e. 2ft 3ins or 2ft 6ins. If you wish to build higher do so, but the idea of the 6in. gap is to allow you to slot the rails into one another if need be — see Photo 15. If you build to a modest height, when you want to set up a jumping lane the heights will not be too formidable.

Obviously the simplest fence will be an upright, but as built there will be no proper groundline and so the starting idea is to set up two hurdles side by side — one a low one and the other a higher one, and put straw bales along the front of them — Fig. 62(a). However long you expect to leave the bales drive a couple of stakes down through them into the ground to prevent them moving, making sure that their tops do not protrude above the bales. This is your basic cross-country fence and you should start off using the low side, encouraging the horse with an approach that is not too fast, but with impulsion. Drive the horse into a restraining hand until you release him just before the take-off stride. Once you have an unhurried, but impulsive, approach and a good effortless bascule over the low hurdle move up to the higher one.

As most cross-country courses will involve gradients it is important to find some slopes where you can build the basic fence and practise jumping it. Firstly uphill, which is the easiest to regulate as all you need to do in most cases is drive on; and secondly, with the bales the other side, downhill (you can of course put bales both sides at the outset).

It is much more difficult to approach a fence correctly when riding downhill as most horses will be thrown onto their forehand and may well refuse to take-off. Flatwork training to lighten the forehand (which is the basis of most of dressage) will teach the horse to get his hocks under him and is an essential pre-requisite to controlled jumping downhill.

If you can build in a woodland setting then be careful to look at the siting of your fences with respect to light and shade. You will want to encourage boldness in your horse so that whatever he meets he can jump without fear as he will accept that you would not put him in jeopardy. Thus it is important in early training not to give him a fright by jumping from sunlight into dark shadow where he cannot see what lies beyond. Riding or leading him into the shadowed part before trying the fence in order to show him that there is no danger is a sensible step and can obviate a nasty refusal.

The same goes for water. You will want to remove any fear of water the horse may have, and if a small stream with a solid bottom presents itself, the basic fence can be set up so that the horse has to jump it into the water. Even a sizeable puddle after rain could be used here, but if the horse is not experienced lead him through the water first to show that he will not disappear into the depths. It also enables you to assess whether or not it is wise to attempt the leap because the quality of the bottom of streams may change with time and while it might once have been good it might have deteriorated.

The line of straw bales makes an easy sloping fence, encouraging the right take-off point, but many fences will not have such aids. So lay a pole along the bottom of the hurdle as the next most difficult alternative. When there are no problems here try a false groundline with, say, a straw-bale oxer, but it is better to have mastered the oxer with a set-forward groundline first.

The bale oxer is a good solid spread fence which will hold itself together naturally and can be made as shown in Fig. 62(b). First of all you can make it into a narrow ascending parallel using a low and a high hurdle sandwiching the bales – Fig. 62(c). You will not really have any problem that the fence has a false groundline here because the bales will provide such a line. Later you can make the fence more problematic by widening it as an ascending fence, and then finally use hurdles of the same height and turn it into a true parallel with a false groundline. (See Photo 17.)

Another way of constructing a simple practice fence is to set up a double-decker line of straw bales and then lean the top rail of one of your hurdles on that. However, as shown in Fig. 62(d) and (e) there is a safe way

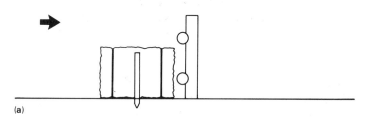

(a)

Fig. 62 *Cross-country fences using hurdles and straw bales.*
(a) *A simple cross-country fence. Stake your bales down and jump this fence only from the direction shown.*

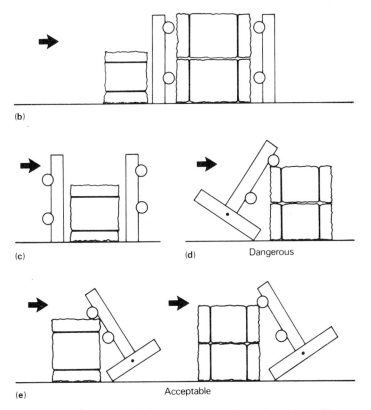

(b) *A more formidable bale oxer. The leading edge bale facilitates jumping and can be removed later.*
(c) *An easy ascending parallel.*

(d) and (e) *Practice fences — acceptable and dangerous.*

and a dangerous way. In (e), if the horse has taken off then his back legs are bound to land beyond the hurdle, but if you set it up as in (d), while it looks an easy sloped fence the novice horse who refuses at the last moment, or makes a puerile attempt at the jump and slides into it, could well trap his legs between the rails.

Photo 17 *A bale oxer.*

Combination Fences

Here are some representative distances to set between hurdles of given height and assuming that the fences are being ridden at a speed of 450 yds/minute which is faster than is normal for show-jumping.

	Fences at 2ft 3ins			Fences at 2ft 9ins			Fences at 3ft 3ins		
number of strides	1	2	3	1	2	3	1	2	3
14.2 hh	20 ft	30	40	21	31	41	23	33	43
15.2 hh	22	33	44	23	34	45	24	36	47
16.2 hh	23	36	49	24	37	50	26	39	52

Where calculation led to half feet appearing in the total lengths these have been rounded up for the shorter distances and down for the longer ones. It is not assumed that 13.2-and-under ponies will habitually jump cross-country. To compute related distances with more strides note the difference between the above and just add this on for each stride.

With cross-country obstacles there are fewer restrictions on what you can construct than there are in show-jumping. A combination obstacle may have two fences at right angles to one another and these may be separated by a rideable distance, or they may be set V-shaped so that you can jump the corner as a spread to save precious seconds.

33 ADDING VARIETY

Making a Bullfinch

A bullfinch is a fence where the brush is so high that the horse has to jump through it, as on steeplechase courses. You can make a bullfinch by placing two of your hurdles close together and binding them together with bale twine or similar. In the slot between the rails you will have to cram the brush (Fig. 63).

Obtaining brush is one of the biggest headaches when you are building at home. What you really want are birch saplings, but you will be hard put to find them. You can use broom providing it is tall enough, but it is essential that whatever you use gives when the horse goes through it and is not going to tear at his legs.

Going to the trouble of finding enough relatively straight saplings or other small branches from the hedgerows — if there are any left in your area — could be worthwhile as the horse might well need considerable encouragement to take this 'blind' fence in his stride and you will have to train him to do it.

You might have to lead the horse into the brush part of the fence by placing poles into it as shown in Fig. 63. Otherwise put show-jumping wings in front to cut down the frontal area and leave only the bull-finch part to be jumped.

Log Piles

Another obstacle you can easily make at home is the log pile. You can use branches from cut-down dead trees or you could even use actual logs that you had bought

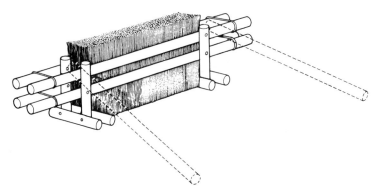

Fig. 63 *Using two rustic hurdles to make a bullfinch fence.*

in for next winter's fire, but make sure they are carefully stacked. Permanent log piles are usually fastened down with rope or wire to fixings driven into the ground, but moderate-sized temporary ones do not really need to be fixed so long as they are carefully constructed. Build a base of hefty and fairly straight branches and build up a prism shape on that.

34 ALTERNATIVE-ROUTE OBSTACLES

Alternative-route obstacles are something you will not find on show-jumping courses. They are multiple-choice fences that can save you valuable seconds if you take the more difficult but direct way through them but which offer another, longer approach and easier going. Photo 18 shows such an obstacle constructed from four hurdles. The coloured flags are placed red on the right and white on the left and the fence must be taken within the flags. How the hurdles are laid out is shown in Fig. 64.

In Photo 18 the route straight across the picture is the direct line of the course and the larger hurdles are employed here. The alternative is ridden from far top left and consists of lower hurdles. The extra distance which you need to ride to approach the alternative correctly and the time involved in regaining the correct track after jumping constitute a distinct disadvantage. The most difficult thing with alternative-route fences is to provide two safe paths, one of which is longer than the other, but is easier to jump. You can get other ideas for such fences from watching horse trials around the country or on TV.

Another thing to do is to make an 'angled combination', that means having two fences both carrying the same number and set at an angle which may be as large as 90°. Thus some strides must be put in to enable the horse to land and turn to negotiate the second part of the obstacle. You will have to put a related distance between the fences. You can find this from page 196.

Photo 18 *An alternative-route obstacle (see also Fig. 64).*

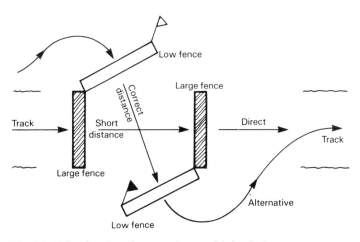

Fig. 64 *Using four hurdles to make a multiple-choice cross-country fence.*

If you number the two fences differently you then have an alternative. You can, if your horse will do it, go in and out on one bend or, if you do not feel your horse can do it, you can land straight, pull up, make a small circle and then jump the second fence. Such a manoeuvre will not be penalised as crossing your own track would be in show-jumping (Fig. 65).

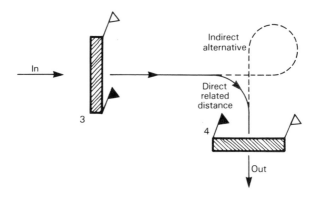

Fig. 65 *Direct and indirect alternative routes allowable in cross-country competitions.*

Using three hurdles, two of which do not actually constitute the fence to be jumped, set in relation to the track as in Fig. 66, gives you three alternatives. The fastest, most direct alternative (a) is to jump the corner just inside the flag as if it were a parallel. Alternative (b) means jumping the low hurdles and the further out from the fence this point is the longer it will take compared to the alternative (a). A well-balanced horse can perhaps take line (b) in three strides whereas a less well-trained one might need five strides. If your horse cannot do either then the slowest route is (c) round the end of the low hurdles and straight out over the fence.

Using four hurdles you can make the obstacles shown

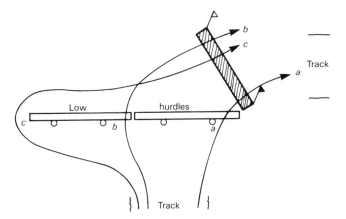

Fig. 66 *This fence offers three alternatives. The bold horse will jump the corner* (a) *or can be taken on a longer route* (b), *making the fence a combination. The novice horse can be ridden round the end of the first hurdle and over the flagged fence* (c).

in Fig. 67 — a formidable parallel on the direct route (*a*), but with an alternative easy route via a longer path (*b*). Another variation on the parallel theme is illustrated in Fig. 68. Here the bigger hurdles are set up so that the gap between them tapers from a 5ft to a 3ft width (or even 2ft if you wish). This gives two of the three alternatives. The third route, easy but much longer, is formed by making a 9ft wide lane of two low hurdles and setting a stile, say on barrel wings, at the end of it. Placed in relation to the track as shown, the horse that jumps big will go straight for the wide part of the parallel (*a*). The horse with less scope may go as far down the tapering parallel as you think he can reasonably clear (*b*). If your horse cannot do either of these then you must jump the stile on the longer track (*c*).

These examples give an idea of the kind of alternatives that might be thought up by cross-country coursebuilders. All fences must be jumped somewhere between

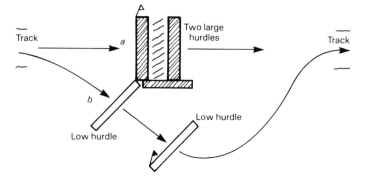

Fig. 67 *An alternative, longer, route* (b) *employs two low hurdles while the higher hurdles are built into a formidable parallel* (a).

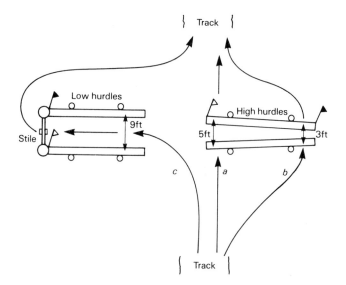

Fig. 68 *Four hurdles and a stile set up to provide a fence with three alternative routes:* (a) *is the direct line but entails a 5ft spread,* (b) *is much less of a spread, while* (c) *is a slow route between the low hurdles and out over the stile.*

the nearest pair of white and red flags (red on the right), e.g. someone might conclude that a bounce into and out of the 9ft width between the low hurdles of the last example was between a white flag on the extreme left and a red flag on the extreme right, but that is not at all what the coursebuilder intended.

35 SLOPING GROUND

A horse ridden downhill will lengthen his stride and one ridden uphill will shorten it. Your paddock may have one or more angles of slope in it and you will find that riding into fences downhill will present many more problems than when jumping uphill. Downhill the horse will be thrown onto his forehand and any problems which arise because the forehand is not developed will be accentuated.

With the lengthened stride you will find it much more difficult to obtain the correct point of take-off, but the problems disappear when the horse has developed some degree of collection. A horse ridden downhill has to be collected whereas when riding uphill he will tend to collect himself. Therefore most of the novice's problems with gradients come when jumping downhill.

The degree of slope need not be great, and a slope of just 5° in the ground radically alters the way in which the fences should be ridden. Only on cross-country courses are you likely to meet slopes of 10° or more which are therefore greater than 1 in 5, but it might be advisable to just set down the principal facts concerning jumping fences up- and downhill.

On a slope the normal stride should be considered to be shortened by 6ins when riding uphill and correspondingly lengthened when riding downhill. Thus two-stride combinations that are to be jumped downhill will need a foot of extra length and they should be correspondingly shortened when going uphill.

When riding uphill the take-off point should increase

in distance from the fence and it will do so rapidly with steepening gradient. The landing distance beyond a fence built on a gradient when coming downhill will increase by some 2ft or more over the same fence built on the flat. These facts are summed up in Fig. 69.

Fig. 69 *How landing and take-off distances change when riding up- and downhill.*

APPENDICES

APPENDIX 1

OFFICIALLY RECOMMENDED DISTANCES

Since the first edition of this book was written the British Show Jumping Association has shortened most of its recommended distances. Thus whereas they were then correct for the largest animals and the kind of heights met with in A and B competitions, the distances now recommended are much more likely to be correct for the majority of riders who are not either professionals or aspiring to be professionals.

The basic distances between uprights for one and two stride combinations in adult competitions now allows for 15.2 to 16.2 hh horses jumping heights between 3ft 3in and 4ft 3in. This is a welcome move because, while the implied stride length of 10ft remains the same for the non-jumping strides, the combined take-off and landing distances have become more reasonable. The pony distances for the same combinations are now reduced to 23ft and 33ft respectively, which is for 13.2 to 14.2 hh animals jumping fences of 4ft or thereabouts. Thus JA ponies or similar are still implied in pony distances. These distances are to be reduced by 6in and a foot respectively for 13.2 and 12.2 hh ponies in both one stride and two stride cases. This latitude allows for the ability of ponies to adjust their stride to meet the situation they meet.

In this book we are considering bringing on novice animals which are not going to be expected to scale 5ft fences. Thus the distances recommended will usually be less than the BSJA figures, but will not now differ a great deal. When 16.2 hh horses and high fences are taken into account the distances in our tables may exceed those recommended by the BSJA. They will be the kind of distances to be found in big money competitions.

I have found that the distances quoted in the foregoing pages work well for local shows and for the stage of training of the horses and riders for whom the book is envisaged. These distances are calculated from the solution of the jumping arc (the bascule) as described in Appendix 2. They allow for the height of the fences being jumped and the speed of approach which is assumed to be slightly less than average (about 390 yd/min). The figures also allow for the shorter strides of smaller animals.

The following is a resumé of the distances currently recommended by the BSJA.

A = upright   B = true parallel   C = ascending parallel
D = triple bar

Horse distances

A—A	24½ft	35ft		C—A	24½ft	35ft
A—B	23½	35		C—B	23	34
A—C	23	35		C—C	22½	33½
A—D	22	33 ✗		C—D	22	33
B—A	24½	35		D—A	25	36
B—B	23	34		D—B	24½	35½
B—C	22½	33½		D—C	24	35½
B—D	22	33 ✗		D—D	Not allowed	

(✗ means not allowed in novice competitions)

In novice competitions or any competition with a first

prize of £50 or over 6in should be added to the one-stride distances. Indoors 6in should be deducted from the one-stride distances.

Pony distances   14.2 hh and under but over 13.2 hh

A—A	23ft	33ft		B—A	23ft	33ft
A—B	22½	33		B—B	⨯	⨯
A—C	22½	33		B—C	⨯	33
				C—A	23	33½
				C—B	⨯	⨯
				C—C	⨯	33

(⨯ means that such combinations are not built and triple bar obstacles are not to be used at all. Six inches are to be taken off these distances for 13.2 hh but over 12.2 hh and 1ft taken off for 12.2 hh ponies.)

Spreads should not exceed the height of the obstacle and in the 12.2 hh and 13.2 hh competitions spread fences are not to be built as second or third elements of combinations. While for JA ponies there are few restrictions for JC and similar competitions spreads can only be used with two-stride doubles or trebles.

APPENDIX 2

THE BASCULE

The bascule of a jumping horse is the path it takes in the air. But what path? The answer is the path of the combined centre of gravity (G) of horse and rider from the moment the last hoof leaves the ground on take-off (S), to when the first hoof comes to the ground on landing (K) (Fig. 70). That path is the same as must be taken by any object in the air with a forward speed and which is then acted on by the force of gravity. It is the path taken by a football when the goalkeeper (or for that matter any player) strikes it up the field. It is the path taken by a shell fired from a gun. From take-off to landing a horse is, in effect, a projectile and as such obeys the laws of projectiles. Technically the shape of the path is a parabola — a very flattened version of the curve of, say, a reflector behind car headlamps or torch bulbs.

Because of the way the horse places his hind feet together on the take-off spot at the same time as he is lowering his hindquarters, the way he enters the free-flight phase is a more or less smooth curve (LJ) that leads into the parabolic shape over the fence. In the same way, because the downward momentum has to be met on landing, that part of the curve (MN) is a smooth curve also.

However the centre of gravity is some 3ft 6ins off the ground for a typical 12.2 hh pony and nearly 5ft for a 17.2 hh horse. So we are following the path of a point that is well off the ground before the horse ever takes off (as in Fig. 70). Then, to conserve his valuable energy,

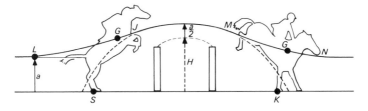

Fig. 70 *What is meant by the 'bascule' — the path taken by the combined centre of gravity of horse and rider.*

the horse tucks his legs up and when he does that the centre of gravity is only about half the above heights above the lowest hoof tip that has to clear the fence.

So in effect the horse does not jump a fence of say, 3ft 6ins, but one which is, as far as the centre of gravity is concerned, less than 3ft 6ins by half the height of his centre of gravity.

Thus a 14.2 hh pony, with a typical height of his centre of gravity of 4ft 4ins from the ground, therefore actually has to raise his bulk only 3ft 6ins minus 2ft 2ins, i.e. 1ft 4ins, and similar considerations apply to any other fence height or horse height. If a 17 hh horse jumps 7ft then he has to raise his mass 4ft 6ins, which does not detract from the feat because calculation shows that the upward speed with which he thrusts off must be comparable to his forward speed.

The path the centre of gravity takes over a fence of effective height H, as measured from actual photographs of horses jumping obstacles, is the line $LJMN$ in Fig. 70. Here S is the true point of take-off, but the horse is raising his centre of gravity before then. Equally K is the point of landing, but the centre of gravity is still well in the air at that time and has to be more or less gently lowered to the ground. The dashed lines are the kind of parabolas you see drawn in books and it shows just what such curves mean. They are lines from near the point of take-off to near the point of landing and which go through the highest point of the bascule.

Once the horse has left the ground nothing you do can affect the shape (*JM*) of the bascule. Leaning forward or back only affects the balance of the horse minutely and certainly not enough to change in any way the path taken by the centre of gravity. Thus shapes of the bascule as drawn in many books which show a different curve on the take-off side to the landing side are not correct. However they may be drawn they are totally diagrammatic as they do not really refer to the line taken by any part of the horse. Drawn symmetrically, as in Fig. 71(a)–(d), they serve to indicate the path of the horse over a fence.

The distances given in the combination section of this book are worked out for a speed of about 400 yards per minute which is considered to be on the slow side of

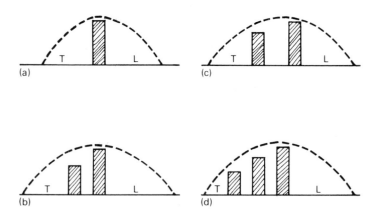

Fig. 71 *The dotted lines serve to indicate the path of the horse over a fence and where, if perfectly jumped, the bascule would come to its zenith.*

an average pace. The speed is about the normal one expected in FEI events when calculating the time allowed and the time limit (the latter is twice the former) and is faster than the normal one expected by the BSJA which is 300 yards per minute. Thus in BSJA events the length of time you have to complete the course without incurring penalties is about a third longer than in FEI events over the same distance.

Once you have established the speed of approach (and assume it is maintained into the point of take-off) and given the height of the horse and the fence, then it is a problem in simple mechanics to work out the distance the horse will cover from take-off to landing. The bascule, however, will not be symmetrical with respect to the fence as it is with the true parallel in Fig. 70.

In Fig. 71 (a) the top of the bascule over an upright is usually just beyond the plane of the fence and as the leading element in (b) does not affect the bascule this fence simply induces the horse to take off further from the main element and so possibly land on it. The 'true' ascending parallel is one where the leading element is high enough to affect the bascule and then the highest point will fall within the spread itself, making the fence effectively higher than it looks. See page 88 (spread coefficients).

The triple bar may also induce a far take-off with subsequent hitting of the main element, but ridden correctly the top of the bascule comes somewhere just inside the main element. Thus in almost all cases the take-off distance T is less than the landing distance L, but the amounts differ from fence to fence. It is these variations which lead to the different values of true distance in the tables.

APPENDIX 3

IMPERIAL/METRIC CONVERSIONS

BRITISH—METRIC CONVERSIONS OF LENGTH

ft.	in.	Decimal ft.	metres	ft.	in.	Decimal ft.	metres	ft.	in.	Decimal ft.	metres
1	0	1.0	0.31	4	0	4.0	1.22	7	0	7.0	2.13
	1	1.1	0.33		1	4.1	1.24		1	7.1	2.16
	2	1.2	0.36		2	4.2	1.27		2	7.2	2.18
	3	1.25	0.38		3	4.25	1.30		3	7.25	2.21
	4	1.3	0.41		4	4.3	1.32		4	7.3	2.24
	5	1.4	0.43		5	4.4	1.35		5	7.4	2.26
	6	1.5	0.46		6	4.5	1.37		6	7.5	2.29
	7	1.6	0.48		7	4.6	1.40		7	7.6	2.31
	8	1.7	0.51		8	4.7	1.42		8	7.7	2.34
	9	1.75	0.53		9	4.75	1.45		9	7.75	2.36
	10	1.8	0.56		10	4.8	1.47		10	7.8	2.39
	11	1.9	0.58		11	4.9	1.50		11	7.9	2.41
2	0	2.0	0.61	5	0	5.0	1.52	8	0	8.0	2.44
	1	2.1	0.64		1	5.1	1.55		1	8.1	2.46
	2	2.2	0.66		2	5.2	1.57		2	8.2	2.49
	3	2.25	0.69		3	5.25	1.60		3	8.25	2.51
	4	2.3	0.71		4	5.3	1.63		4	8.3	2.54
	5	2.4	0.74		5	5.4	1.65		5	8.4	2.57
	6	2.5	0.76		6	5.5	1.68		6	8.5	2.59
	7	2.6	0.79		7	5.6	1.70		7	8.6	2.62
	8	2.7	0.82		8	5.7	1.73		8	8.7	2.64
	9	2.75	0.84		9	5.75	1.75		9	8.75	2.67
	10	2.8	0.87		10	5.8	1.78		10	8.8	2.69
	11	2.9	0.89		11	5.9	1.80		11	8.9	2.72
3	0	3.0	0.91	6	0	6.0	1.83	9	0	9.0	2.74
	1	3.1	0.94		1	6.1	1.85		1	9.1	2.77
	2	3.2	0.97		2	6.2	1.88		2	9.2	2.80
	3	3.25	0.99		3	6.25	1.90		3	9.25	2.82
	4	3.3	1.02		4	6.3	1.93		4	9.3	2.84
	5	3.4	1.04		5	6.4	1.96		5	9.4	2.86
	6	3.5	1.07		6	6.5	1.98		6	9.5	2.89
	7	3.6	1.10		7	6.6	2.01		7	9.6	2.92
	8	3.7	1.12		8	6.7	2.03		8	9.7	2.95
	9	3.75	1.14		9	6.75	2.06		9	9.75	2.97
	10	3.8	1.17		10	6.8	2.08		10	9.8	2.99
	11	3.9	1.19		11	6.9	2.11		11	9.9	3.02

BRITISH—METRIC CONVERSIONS OF LENGTH

ft.	in.	Decimal ft.	metres	ft.	in.	Decimal ft.	metres	ft.	in.	Decimal ft.	metres
10	0	10.0	3.05	13	0	13.0	3.97	16	0	16.0	4.88
	1	10.1	3.08		1	13.1	4.00		1	16.1	4.91
	2	10.2	3.10		2	13.2	4.02		2	16.2	4.93
	3	10.25	3.12		3	13.25	4.04		3	16.25	4.95
	4	10.3	3.15		4	13.3	4.06		4	16.3	4.97
	5	10.4	3.17		5	13.4	4.08		5	16.4	5.00
	6	10.5	3.20		6	13.5	4.11		6	16.5	5.03
	7	10.6	3.23		7	13.6	4.14		7	16.6	5.06
	8	10.7	3.26		8	13.7	4.17		8	16.7	5.09
	9	10.75	3.28		9	13.75	4.19		9	16.75	5.11
	10	10.8	3.30		10	13.8	4.21		10	16.8	5.13
	11	10.9	3.32		11	13.9	4.24		11	16.9	5.16
11	0	11.0	3.35	14	0	14.0	4.27				
	1	11.1	3.38		1	14.1	4.30				
	2	11.2	3.41		2	14.2	4.33				
	3	11.25	3.43		3	14.25	4.35				
	4	11.3	3.45		4	14.3	4.37				
	5	11.4	3.47		5	14.4	4.39				
	6	11.5	3.50		6	14.5	4.42				
	7	11.6	3.53		7	14.6	4.45				
	8	11.7	3.56		8	14.7	4.48				
	9	11.75	3.58		9	14.75	4.50				
	10	11.8	3.60		10	14.8	4.52				
	11	11.9	3.63		11	14.9	4.55				
12	0	12.0	3.66	15	0	15.0	4.57				
	1	12.1	3.69		1	15.1	4.60				
	2	12.2	3.72		2	15.2	4.63				
	3	12.25	3.74		3	15.25	4.65				
	4	12.3	3.76		4	15.3	4.67				
	5	12.4	3.79		5	15.4	4.70				
	6	12.5	3.81		6	15.5	4.73				
	7	12.6	3.84		7	15.6	4.76				
	8	12.7	3.87		8	15.7	4.79				
	9	12.75	3.89		9	15.75	4.81				
	10	12.8	3.91		10	15.8	4.83				
	11	12.9	3.94		11	15.9	4.85				

Conversions are given from feet and inches into decimal feet and into metres. Values are given up to 17ft so that for most combination distances just doubling one of the conversion figures will give the true distance in metres.

INDEX